Guilt Free

life

Guilt Free

Reclaiming Your Life from
Unreasonable Expectations

Jennifer Reid, MD

· PENGUIN LIFE

VIKING
An imprint of Penguin Random House LLC
1745 Broadway, New York, NY 10019
penguinrandomhouse.com

A Penguin Life Book

Designed by Alexis Sulaimani

ISBN 9780593833469 (hardcover)
ISBN 9780593833476 (ebook)

Printed in the United States of America
1st Printing

The authorized representative in the EU for product safety and compliance
is Penguin Random House Ireland, Morrison Chambers, 32 Nassau
Street, Dublin D02 YH68, Ireland, https://eu-contact.penguin.ie.

For my mother, my grandmothers,
and all of the other extraordinary women in my life.

You've inspired me to raise my voice.

Contents

Author's Note

Guilt Free highlights strategies to help women better recognize and begin to lower their excessive guilt, utilizing an inclusive definition of woman. The recommendations and techniques reflect some of the unique challenges people who identify as women face in their daily lives, but they are certainly not limited to any one gender or group. I welcome all readers to these pages and hope you find something useful in the book.

As you read, you will hear stories of women who are struggling with excessive guilt. Though they certainly represent aspects of the lived experiences of women I've treated in my psychiatry practice, confidentiality is very important in my work. Therefore, I have created fictional composites, rather than incorporating personal details, to protect my patients' privacy.

Lastly, the information is designed to provide support and education, but it cannot serve as a replacement for medical care and is not intended to diagnose, treat, cure, or prevent any condition or disease. If you have questions or concerns about your own health, please contact your health care provider.

Introduction

Nora sits across from me in my office, staring out the window, shaking her head and smiling. Though I am curious, I decide not to ask any questions, instead giving her some time to tell me what is on her mind.

Minutes pass. Finally, she turns to me.

"I think the only time I don't feel guilty is when I'm sleeping."

Here we are. Highly functional, engaging, compassionate women, navigating the complexities of romantic relationships, parenthood, careers, our aging parents, and our own identity. Even as you read this, these incredibly challenging endeavors demand your attention, energy, and time, which you give throughout each hectic day. And yet, in my sessions, I hear the same question over and over again.

Why do I feel so guilty all the time?

My psychiatry practice supports women during each stage of life, from first love and leaving home, to the overwhelming responsibility of parenting and the stress of building a career, all the way through the grief of slowly declining health in our friends and partners in late life. I've seen excessive guilt show up in different ways across all these important stages, universally robbing women of their enthusiasm and joy. Guilt makes us believe that the reason we're falling short is because we're not giving it our all or trying hard enough. But the reality is, we're not falling short. We're already giving so much. It is our expectations that are to blame, suggesting anything short of perfection is a failure. The myth of the "perfect" woman—thoughtful friend, attentive mother, present partner, capable in every way—is unattainable, but that doesn't stop many of us from trying to become her, and from feeling guilty when we inevitably fall short. Influenced by our expectations, we think, "If only I do this thing better, I will feel good about myself."

Yes, *if only* you remember everyone's birthday, anniversary, and latest hobby or crafting obsession and be the perfect friend. *If only* you could avoid sugar all day and then cook healthy, vitamin-rich meals every night. *If only* you could somehow triple the hours in the day to finish the project your boss dropped onto your desk at the last minute. Yes, you may feel miserable or believe you are lacking now, but the future will be different— *if only* you just try harder!

As I continue my session with Nora, she describes how overwhelmed she's felt this past month. First, her mother has been hospitalized with a foot infection and now calls Nora several times a day because she is lonely, but with Nora's busy schedule, she isn't always available to answer. Then her daughter brings home a low score on a math quiz and says, "I think boys really are better with numbers." Nora now feels guilty not only for her daughter's challenges but also for not protecting her from absorbing this idea that girls can't do math. ("Ugh. Where did I go so wrong?") On top of everything, Nora's work responsibilities have increased significantly after a colleague abruptly left, but she hasn't received additional support or higher pay. Instead of asking for help, she blames her lack of time-management skills for her overflowing workload.

I think we can all relate to Nora when she describes feeling like she is falling behind in one area as soon as she turns her attention to something else. Nora, like so many of us, is drowning in the expectations that come with being a woman trying to navigate multiple competing roles, viewing each day as a series of tasks for completion rather than a chance to find meaning and joy. She blames herself when loved ones seem unhappy, thinking she must be doing something wrong. She feels guilty if she doesn't exercise or eat right, criticizing herself for her "lack of control." She is inundated by unreasonable expectations placed on her in her job. Through it all, she accuses herself of not working hard enough to avoid falling behind. She's even felt guilty when she's tried to get help in the past, blaming herself for not feeling better.

So there it is again: guilt.

Introduction

In several ways, guilt can be a helpful emotion, which you are evolutionarily wired to feel. It helps you create and nurture healthy relationships, allows you to demonstrate your commitment to others, and guides you toward repair when you've made a mistake. Without guilt, connecting with others would be harder. However, this adaptive type of guilt is not what you will be learning about in this book.

The guilt I'm describing is the opposite of helpful, because it is excessive. It has surpassed its evolutionary utility for connection and instead fuels self-criticism, thoughts of failure and inadequacy, sadness and overwhelm, even depression and other health problems. It drives your decision-making and generates unhealthy behaviors like perfectionism, people-pleasing, and self-denial, creating a cycle of suffering. You might agree to an activity you absolutely hate, rather than experience the guilt of saying no. You turn down concert tickets to see your favorite band because you feel guilty asking your neighbor to swing by and let your dog out while you're away. You suffer through a miserable day at work with a terrible cold because you don't want to let your coworkers down. Guilt repeatedly asks us, "What makes you think you're worthwhile when you're not achieving or producing? Why would others want to spend time with you if you aren't perfect? Why can't you do anything *right*?"

But that's the lie we're all telling ourselves.

Many of us view this critical voice as a necessary evil, pushing us toward becoming a better person—because guilt is a pretty effective motivator. By threatening yourself with criticism and disappointment, you might make it to the gym or schedule that dental appointment. Guilt also offers an enticing illusion of control. You may believe you've messed up, but if you just work harder, you can fix it, right?

But guilt also blocks your access to joy and pleasure. You "indulge" in something truly pleasurable, such as an ice cream cone on a warm day or a relaxing massage after a busy week. Instead of savoring it, you feel guilty for your lack of self-control or selfish desire to take time for yourself, ruining this brief interlude of joy. Guilt, then, becomes the payment for any moment of satisfaction you dare to experience for yourself.

When you start exploring the reasons for this excessive guilt, for these moments when you judge your attempts to rest and take pleasure, berate yourself for your imperfections, or seem to accumulate never-ending tasks and responsibilities, you can quickly hit a brick wall, thinking, "I just don't understand why I'm always feeling this way."

I know what it feels like to live with excessive guilt and I'm guessing you do, too. For a long time, I struggled with this constant feeling. Despite my education and training, it still seemed like guilt was in control. I'd be going about my day, trying to care for my patients, my family, maybe even myself, and bam! There it was again, telling me I was lazy and undisciplined: guilt. Guilt urged me to do more and judge myself for periods of rest, reflection, and even sadness. It reared its ugly head every time I experienced frustration or impatience with my kids, because I worried that meant I wasn't appreciating our time together enough, even when my frustration was totally warranted. ("I should enjoy taking them grocery shopping, even when they run over my heel with the cart.")

When your guilt tells you to quiet your wishes because your needs are less important than others' or suggests you matter only if you are optimally productive, attractive, or taking care of others, these are all lies. Guilt is responsible for this brutal voice in your head telling you you're never enough. This is why, friends, I am *done* with all this guilt, and I hope you are, too. If you find yourself thinking, "There has to be a better way," you're absolutely right.

If you, like Nora and like so many of us, live with guilt as your everyday experience, I know I can help you find relief, for the following reasons:

1. I've studied the brain and human behavior for more than a decade, as a board-certified psychiatrist and in my role as an academic physician, teaching future doctors at premier institutions around the country. I know how to make changes in your unhelpful thoughts and actions.

2. I've sought out the best research on the development and management of our most difficult emotions, especially guilt.

3. I wrote this book to figure out *my own* difficult relationship with guilt, and it has helped me enormously.

4. I've helped thousands of women finally stop letting guilt run their lives, allowing them to make decisions based on their true desires and goals.

Guilt Free is a guide to understanding and letting go of your guilt, so you can start living according to what you want and need instead of what you think you should be doing. We'll start by examining the mechanisms of guilt, exploring how some guilt is good and even necessary; the origins of our most debilitating expectations; and key reasons guilt can be so difficult to relinquish. Then, we'll dive into the how. The process of lowering our guilt begins with noticing the expectations that are subconsciously driving us; by identifying our guilt triggers. We'll explore how to lower the noise of our loudest guilty thoughts and learn techniques to shift to a better way of making important decisions with agency rather than guilt or criticism. Along the way, I'll share brief stories representing the thousands of women I've helped in my practice over the years, giving you a glimpse into the lives of women who are also struggling with guilt.

Change is possible when you learn how to understand yourself and can then make informed choices about your life. By the end of the book, my hope is that these choices will be guided by many things—joy, desire, grief, a craving for mint chocolate chip ice cream, even anger—but they will no longer be controlled by guilt. It doesn't mean you will never feel guilty or any number of other difficult emotions. You will just be empowered to choose the path that you want to follow, rather than the one you believe you *should*.

Let's learn to identify and neutralize guilty thoughts, treat ourselves with kindness, approach setbacks as learning experiences rather than failures, and recognize our many contributions.

Welcome, friends, to a life with less guilt!

Guilt
Free

1.

Understanding Guilt

We seem to be doing all right, but I still feel like such a failure," Janine tells me. When I ask for examples of how she is failing, she quickly launches into a long list of ways she believes she is letting people down.

"I haven't finished the paperwork for my new employees to get health insurance," she begins. "I never see my husband because he has such a long commute and I usually work in the evenings, when he's home. My mother is more connected to my daughter than I am, since she watches her while I'm at the office all day. I pay for this expensive gym and never go. My daughter had a huge tantrum in the grocery store last week when I was just trying to grab a few things and I ended up bribing her with candy, which I know is terrible."

She then asks me, "Why do I feel so guilty all the time? I'm tired of being this frustrated and exhausted, but I don't know how to change it."

Haven't we all felt this way at some point, our emotions overpowering us with their sudden intensity? You may sometimes wish you could simply cut them off completely, seeking relief from their powerful influences on your mind and body. However, they represent a crucial part of your survival—yes, even the tough ones, like guilt.

Adaptive Guilt

Emotions can be divided into two main categories. First, there are the primary or basic emotions—like fear, anger, joy, and sadness—that serve essential survival functions, like helping us recognize the difference between a safe environment and one that might be dangerous. Then we have the secondary or social emotions, which include embarrassment, jealousy, empathy, and, yes, guilt. These emotions are prosocial because they help support our relationships and ability to work with others. They not only involve our individual experiences but also occur *in relation to* others.[1]

Think about it. Embarrassment may not feel good in the moment, but it allows us to adjust and reconnect if we've overstepped or made some kind of social blunder. Jealousy, another aversive emotion, signals that we care about someone enough to respond passionately to the threat of loss or unmasks a secret desire we've hidden from ourselves. Empathy helps us to better understand others' experiences and emotions, allowing a deeper social connection. Guilt works the same way.

We are evolutionarily wired to feel guilt. Without guilt, it would be much more difficult to form and strengthen our most important relationships. Interpersonal guilt—guilt that arises in our interactions with others—is adaptive because it is helpful for forging connection. It does so in three distinct ways:[2]

1. **Expressing Care.** First, guilt allows one member of a couple or group to express care and commitment in the face of wrongdoing. Essentially, in order to experience guilt, you must feel some kind of connection to the other people involved.
   "I feel guilty for letting you down because I care about you."

2. **Rebalancing Inequities.** Second, guilt serves to fix or rebalance inequities in emotional distress within the relationship, meaning if your partner does something wrong but later feels guilty about it, then at least *both* of you will feel equally bad in the end. Additionally, this is how guilt can provide an important motivation for repair after a big fight.

"I feel so guilty for hurting her feelings. This is awful. I need to do something to make her feel better."

3. **Influencing Others.** Third, guilt provides a way for one individual or group, especially those from positions of lesser power, to influence the other. By evoking guilt in the more powerful person or group, the less powerful individual can sway them to make desired changes.

"I wish your organization would be willing to help us raise money for our local food bank, but I guess it's not a priority for you this year."

As you can see, not all guilt is bad. In fact, our ability to experience the reparative motivation that guilt provides has allowed us as a species to succeed at a level far beyond most of our closest relatives in the animal kingdom.[3] We can connect and collaborate in such highly sophisticated ways because our distant ancestors who were best at feeling and responding to these social emotions were the ones who survived and passed along their genetic information.

One of the reasons for this is because guilt works closely with another vital social emotion: empathy. Guilt and empathy work together in important ways. If we are able to truly understand what someone else is feeling through the illuminating process of feeling it ourselves, *and* we believe we are somehow responsible for causing that feeling, we will experience a powerful motivation to attempt repair. This is why a sincere "I'm sorry" from a loved one tempers your anger and eases your hurt. It shows you that they understand your pain, maybe even feel it themselves, and care enough to try to make you feel better. This type of interaction leads to increased communication and collaboration—and collaboration is always an evolutionarily adaptive outcome.

While we are all born with the biological ability to feel these social emotions, researchers have found that guilt and empathy truly begin to take shape around age three. This evolutionary legacy is learned and enhanced over time through your interactions with others, as well as through the direct teaching of your parents and other role models. As a child's brain begins to mature, they develop the ability to recognize they are not the only person on earth—which, if you've ever tried to convince a three-year-old to share their toys, you know can be tricky. Around this time, they are also learning the difference between right and wrong, which is shaped by their interactions with the world around them. In the process, they're beginning to understand that when bad things happen to someone else, it might be because of something they have done. This is when repair skills can be taught. Infants, on the other hand, are not able to comprehend these dynamics. They just know how to cry when they are hungry, wet, or tired. The ability to experience both guilt and empathy is thought to create our conscience, an important part of our lives as caring, connected individuals. Therefore, think about how much we must learn in our earliest years—all this complicated information can be put together by age three. (Human brains are incredible, aren't they?)

However, when guilt is used as the primary tool to influence or control behavior—even in theoretically adaptive ways—it becomes maladaptive.

Maladaptive Guilt

Unlike adaptive guilt, maladaptive guilt is not conducive to collaboration or strengthening relationships. In fact, it can have a number of negative interpersonal consequences, including distancing you from your loved ones and creating unnecessary conflict. Also, as we will discuss throughout this book, when we use maladaptive guilt to influence or control ourselves, we become burdened with an overwhelming sense of never doing enough.

Let's start with maladaptive guilt turned outward, or manipulative guilt. This is the use of guilt to influence someone in an unfair or overwhelming way; in other words, to manipulate. Because guilt, especially when forced on you by someone else, is very uncomfortable, it may provide a short-term benefit—you end up doing what the other person would like you to do, and they might feel cared for in the moment— but it doesn't always create the long-term change they desire, which is increased connection. If you've experienced someone using guilt as a mechanism of control, you know very well there are risks to this method. You naturally avoid things that make you feel awful, and if someone is making you feel awful through guilt, you may begin to significantly limit your time with them.

Consider Carolyn, who resides alone in an assisted-living facility. During a visit from her adult daughter, she realizes she would like to see more of her but struggles with mobility and cannot regularly travel to her daughter's home. Carolyn believes she can no longer directly tell her daughter what to do, now that she is a grown woman. However, she would still like to influence her daughter's decisions. By inducing her daughter's guilt with statements such as, "It's nice to finally have you here to see me. I know you're usually too busy to make the trip," she may be able to motivate her daughter to act according to her wishes—to visit more, in this case. Additionally, if she senses her daughter is feeling guilty about not meeting her needs, Carolyn can also be reassured that her daughter still cares about her (the first prosocial effect of adaptive guilt).

Let's pause for a moment to consider Carolyn's approach. Does she realize she's using guilt to manipulate her daughter? It's possible. Perhaps she has consciously shifted to this strategy after years of failed attempts to control her independent daughter's choices. Alternatively, she may not recognize her words are creating guilt for her daughter. This may just have been her dynamic with her own mother and she's repeating history, unconsciously evoking the same emotions she may have felt as a younger woman. In the end, it may not matter. The effect on her daughter is still a negative one—and ultimately leads to fewer visits and less time together, a painful distancing neither wants.

Contrast this with a more direct approach Carolyn could take. She could tell her daughter she feels lonely and really enjoys when she visits. They could then have a conversation about different ways Carolyn might be able to connect with others when her daughter is not there, and how to increase her interactions with her daughter, even if her daughter can't always visit in person. In other words, this kind of honest communication is more likely to help Carolyn meet her needs, including a closer connection with her loving daughter.

Remember, manipulative guilt might seem helpful in the short term, but over time, using it to elicit care and influence behavior ultimately leads to a loss of connection and a buildup of resentment, and everyone misses out. Guilt, then, is usually not the best way to influence your partners and loved ones. It's also not the best way to influence yourself.

The Guilt Equation: When Guilt Turns Inward

The other form of maladaptive guilt, and the primary focus of this book, is the guilt you direct at yourself. It emerges when you believe you've done something wrong—the key word here being *believe*. This is an important aspect of guilt: It is *not* always based on fact. Rather than responding to a situation based on what's actually happening, you measure yourself against a broad set of expectations to see if you make the grade. And if and when you don't, guilt creeps in, regardless of whether that expectation was realistic in the first place.

There are many factors that play into our daily experiences of excessive guilt. The more I've researched, however, the more I've realized you can simplify all of them to these two variables:

What you expect of yourself

How well you believe you are meeting these expectations

That's it. That's the Guilt Equation.

Guilt = Expectations - Reality

The Guilt Equation is a powerful framework for understanding—and ultimately dismantling—the roots of our excessive guilt. Remember, as with all your emotions, guilt—even maladaptive guilt—is a signal. In the same way an accidental splash of boiling water creates a burning sting on your skin, your emotions are a response to your environment and what you believe about your environment. They alert you to your surrounding world and can help you identify how events and experiences are affecting you. When you find yourself buried under an overwhelming amount of guilt, you can begin using the Guilt Equation to uncover your deeply held, often unreasonable expectations, and to shift your attention to your many hidden gifts and contributions. Excessive guilt arises when your expectations vastly outmatch your perception of reality.

First, let's define some terms. What exactly do I mean by *expectations?* Expectations are the beliefs you carry about each of the roles you hold. They are shaped by broad forces, including societal pressure (such as social media displays of unrealistic parenthood or beliefs about women's "natural place" in the world); your most important relationships (like your partner's belief that you are the one who always keeps track of things); your family of origin (such as the way your mother and father divided household and caretaking duties); even your own core beliefs (like perfection is the only path to love and acceptance). Your expectations are the standards you subconsciously try to meet—and feel guilty about when you don't.

For example, if your expectation of being a good colleague means being available for any last-minute project, never complaining if you aren't given the credit you deserve, and regularly sacrificing your personal life to "hop on a quick work call," then your guilt rises the further your true activities depart from this ideal. If, instead, you set reachable expectations for yourself in the workplace, the guilt may begin to lessen. Maybe you remind your supervisor of her promise to hold off on work calls after hours or you ask a colleague to add your name to a presentation you spent hours helping him create, so the team knows how hard you've been working. Learning how to shift your outsize, unhelpful expectations is a powerful way to lower your guilt.

Which brings us to the other variable: our perception of reality—*perception* being the key word here. The Guilt Equation uses your subjective version of reality, meaning what you believe, rather than one based on absolute fact. This is because, like many of us, you may tend to have a really skewed view of your everyday accomplishments and capabilities.

Let's compare this tendency to overlook our efforts to the process of taring the small kitchen scale used for precise baking measurements. After you place a small bowl on the scale, you push the tare button to reset the scale before adding flour or other dry ingredients. The weight of the bowl is now magically *zero*. Often, women use this same process to negate the positive things we are doing in our lives. You view yourself as a terrible person after missing one call from a struggling friend, even though you've spent the past week bringing her little gifts and texting her positive messages. At work, you ignore all the positive things your supervisor told you in your latest job review, focusing instead on the one recent deadline you had to extend. Your accomplishments disappear to zero as you focus instead on what you *haven't* done and potential you *haven't* met.

When your accomplishments and efforts are overlooked, the reality variable of the Guilt Equation drops precipitously. All you are left with are those sky-high expectations, leading to similarly outsize experiences of guilt. What this means is that doing more may not lower your guilt; instead, you need to acknowledge the countless amazing things you are *already* doing every single day. Getting three kids fed, dressed, and off to school. Planning an entire bridal shower for your friend. Working a twelve-hour day to finish a big project in time for an unexpected meeting. These are all major accomplishments. Give yourself some credit where credit is due.

You may be incredibly skilled at spotting the ways you believe you are falling short, but lowering your excessive guilt requires you to make a crucial shift in focus. Ask yourself, "What am I already doing that's amazing?" When I encourage this reframe of your current reality, I'm not saying you just need to pretend everything is great. Life will throw challenges at you every single day, and you will, understandably, be affected by them. Instead, I'm suggesting you try to view your life through new, more accurate eyes. What is currently true? With this shift in perspective, you might be surprised by the many things you are already doing well.

Consider the following dramatic example of the effects of unreasonable expectations and overlooked accomplishments. During the height of the COVID-19 pandemic, when we were all adjusting to a massive, once-in-a-lifetime cultural shift, many of us felt guilty for being less productive at work, having a messier house, feeling impatient with our children, making fewer healthy food choices, or not exercising as often as we thought we should. Many women described feeling a pressure to use their time well, whatever that means, often responding to the performative social media influencers and their smelly sourdough starters or entrepreneurial ventures.

What we magically removed from our perception of reality, however, was our incredible flexibility as we responded to confusing recommendations, protecting ourselves, along with our friends and families, from a novel and dangerous virus. We were able to adjust to online communication for all things and make it through each day in the absence of our usual support system and social interactions. What a feat! These courageous adaptations, and others like them, must be acknowledged in our perception of reality. Otherwise, we get excessive guilt.

It's not just the major efforts, like responding to a disaster, that need to be acknowledged. Every single day, you are doing so many important things, even if they seem small. You're facing the challenges each of your roles provides, whether it's getting dressed and ready for the day even when you didn't sleep well, preparing for a meeting that you're dreading, taking bathtime duties with your kids even though you know you'll get soaked in the process, or driving a friend to the airport because her ride fell through. Take a few moments each evening to look back on the day's activities. You might be surprised by just how much you've accomplished.

Can you stop letting guilt make your decisions? Will you be able to rewrite these tired scripts you've carried around for so many years that tell you to keep doing more and to work harder, convincing you that what you've been doing is simply not enough? Absolutely.

Learning to view guilt as a helpful signal gives you an important opportunity to observe it with curiosity rather than judgment.

How Guilt Hijacks Our Decision-Making

Amanda came to my office following a major argument with her mother that caused her mother to refuse to return Amanda's calls, which she found highly upsetting. I asked her to share a little more about their relationship. At first, she was highly complimentary, but as she continued to share details, a pattern began to emerge.

Amanda noticed she tried to anticipate what her mother might like and then adjusted her choices accordingly. She was trying to be a good daughter, and to her that meant always being available for her mother and avoiding any choices that might upset her. When her mother had a bad fall, Amanda took time off work—despite it being a stressful period—to join her for every medical appointment. When her mother asked to get coffee or lunch last-minute, she always said yes, even if it meant canceling plans with her friends, telling herself, "It's my mom, I need to spend time with her because she's getting older." And when she was too exhausted from work or traveling to say yes to her mother's invitations, she felt so guilty, she ended up avoiding saying anything and instead didn't reach out for several days. Unsurprisingly, the avoidance only amplified the guilt.

Eventually, Amanda began to tell me about the recent argument with her mother. Her mom had planned a family dinner at her home, and without telling Amanda, she had invited the single son of a friend, hoping he and Amanda might hit it off. In the past, Amanda had repeatedly asked her mother to stay out of her love life, but eventually she gave up. Her mother simply wouldn't listen. So when her mom pulled her aside to ask what she thought of the visiting man, Amanda, boiling over with resentment, lashed out.

"I should have given him a chance," she told me. "My mom was just trying to be helpful. I said some awful things to her, and now I feel absolutely terrible. No wonder she won't return my calls. I shouldn't have lost my temper with her. If I could have just gotten through the dinner, we wouldn't have fought."

Excessive guilt, when left unchecked, eventually takes over your decision-making system and sense of self. Instead of making choices based on what you want and need, you make them based on what you think you should be doing in order to be a good daughter, mother, colleague, partner, person, [fill in the blank]. This may alleviate the discomfort of your guilt in the moment, reinforcing this approach. However, in the long run, it will only make your life worse. Instead of thoughtfully responding to a situation or request, you will let guilt pressure you into overscheduling an already busy week or agreeing to activities you would much rather skip. Guilt will tell you that you've failed if you forget one task on your endless list or miss one trip to the gym. Or like it did with Amanda, guilt will lead you to live in a state of perpetual disappointment. In other words, if you are living under the influence of constant guilt, you aren't allowing yourself to be human, with human moments of imperfection.

This is one of the biggest costs of excessive guilt. Doing things you don't actually want to do over and over again simply because to not do them would mean disappointment in others only breeds resentment and dread, even avoidance. This is simply not a sustainable way to live. Yet many of us get caught in the cycle of trying to be the Ideal Woman—and the Ideal Woman does not disappoint others. Yes, Amanda's mother often crossed boundaries and disregarded Amanda's wishes. But in her attempt to meet the unreasonable expectations of being a "good" daughter, Amanda was neglecting her own needs and desires, and telling herself she wasn't allowed to feel frustrated or upset, even though these emotions were warranted. Over time, this kind of suppression can lead to sudden outbursts of emotional expression—often in ways you would prefer to avoid—and can cause demoralization, physical and emotional depletion, and a loss of self-efficacy.

Also, because time is not a renewable resource, letting guilt push you into activities or responsibilities you don't enjoy, or even feel uncomfortable doing, means you have less time in your life for the many things you actually want to do. Perhaps guilt forces you out of bed even though you need more rest to recover from a bad cold or recent travel. You might look at your calendar for the week and because you've felt too guilty to say no, it's so crammed with tasks and responsibilities that you don't have time to pick up groceries, forcing you to rely on takeout and spend money you were hoping to save. In this way, guilt actually creates limitations and disappointment in your life, which is a costly trade-off.

Guilt Versus Shame

Before we move on, it's important to differentiate guilt from another difficult feeling that can affect us in similar ways: shame. Guilt and shame are alike in many ways. They're both highly uncomfortable to experience. They can elicit negative thoughts and behaviors and be used to manipulate others and ourselves. But the difference lies in the root of the emotion. While guilt is a voice within you saying, "I've *done* something wrong," shame proclaims, "I *am* wrong." While guilt arises after a particular behavior, shame occurs when the focus is on the entire self.[4] What this means is that inherently, guilt can be adaptive, whereas shame more often is not.

Guilt, as we've learned, can be socially beneficial. When you do something you wish you hadn't, guilt drives you to make things right. Shame, on the other hand, is like a black mold that flourishes in the darkness; rather than triggering repair, it can cause you to pull away, hide, deny, or try to escape the situation. As a result, once shame is evoked, it can be very difficult to continue to connect with others. If you are triggered to feel shame—to believe you are flawed in a deep and pervasive way—you may retreat, assuming rejection even when there is none. Or you may create masks for public consumption, hiding your authentic self behind the protective covering of indifference or performative self-assurance. At first, the mask might work, but there is always a cost. If you believe those who choose your company might not do so if they knew the "real you," it can be difficult to form intimate relationships with confidence. This can lead to cycles of conflict and misunderstanding, preventing you from feeling truly connected or supported.

Unfortunately, the world primes many of us for shame in what it perpetuates about race, culture, religion, social status, and family of origin. You may have spent years believing you were less valuable or lovable because you grew up with a different skin color, spiritual belief, or level of financial means from those you perceived modeled the "correct" way to be. This shame, then, can lead to social isolation, fear of intimacy, or lower self-confidence in your adult life.

Shame is simply not an adaptive emotion, often causing you to pull away or hide yourself from the world, and burdening you with self-critical and painful beliefs. In fact, the best policy is to recognize it when it shows up, and then send it packing, reminding yourself it's just spreading lies. When it comes to guilt, however, yes, excessive amounts can really interfere with our lives, as we will discuss further in the coming chapters, but in some cases, appropriate guilt can be adaptive and help to nurture strong social relationships.

As we prepare to move on to the next chapter, remember, guilt isn't inherently bad. In fact, it can help you demonstrate to others that you care about them, and allow you to repair after an argument or other difficult conflict. In other words, in some situations, it can be adaptive.

However, when the amount of guilt continues to escalate and you begin to turn it inward, battering yourself with guilt about your responses to your environments, stressors, and experiences, it can just make everything harder. Thankfully, it's possible to let go of all this ugly, overwhelming guilt. You can begin by approaching your guilt as a signal, one that points you to all the ways you're downplaying your abilities and contributions, as well as to the many unreasonable expectations driving your choices. Because, unfortunately, there are many, many expectations today's society asks women to accept.

2.

Why Do Women Experience So Much Guilt?

L et me begin this chapter by exposing a fundamental source of women's excessive guilt. Maybe you've sensed its influence but didn't know how to describe it. Fortunately, my role as a psychiatrist has allowed me to spend more than a decade speaking with women just like you. Over and over, until I couldn't deny its powerful truth, I heard examples of how women are programmed to move through the world in a certain way: Since childhood, many of us have been taught and then relentlessly driven to set unreachable, overwhelming expectations for ourselves—and then to feel guilty when we inevitably fall short.

What I'm talking about is socialization.

The Power of Socialization

You were not born feeling guilty. As we learned in chapter 1, children develop the capacity to feel guilt around age three, when they're starting to socialize with others and beginning to learn how to empathize, repair, and connect. As you approached adulthood, however, society started expecting more from you, and these expectations were reinforced by a huge number of influences: your parents and first caretakers, your friends, partners, and bosses, your schools and communities, and eventually yourself. Socialization is the cumulative effect of all these influences, the way you have been raised within a particular time and culture, as well as how these learned expectations have been reinforced throughout your lifetime.[1]

Everyone experiences socialization, but there are few more powerful scripts than those around gender. Although girls and women today have more opportunities for careers and other activities than in the past, women are still raised—and expected—to be patient, socially aware, and caring, even at the expense of our own ambitions, while boys are more commonly taught to be assertive and strong leaders. Like many women, from a young age, you may have been asked to take on childcare and household duties more regularly than the male children in your family. You may have been taught to take responsibility for others, including their emotions. For example, research suggests if we perceive someone is upset, it is more likely to feel like a threat to our relationship than it may seem to men in a similar situation.[2]

What happens is that over time, we learn that there is an Ideal Woman, and to be her is to be highly responsible, constantly caretaking, and completely selfless. To not be her is to fail. This is one reason socialization can be so powerful, because of the reward that comes when you adhere to your prescribed expectations—and the penalty that comes when you don't. If you attend your child's every school bake sale and soccer practice, volunteer for carpool, and pack your kid's lunch every morning—even though you could use some much-needed rest after an intense week—you may be viewed as a "good mother." But if you miss a school event because you wanted to spend those hours reading a new book or if you forget to send the kids to school in the proper spirit week attire, you are judged harshly, especially by yourself.

This pressure is present for women everywhere. At work, for instance, in addition to taking on the projects your job requires, you may also be asked to take on invisible labor, such as planning the holiday party, taking notes in meetings, or organizing the office supplies. If you turn down these tasks, colleagues may complain you aren't a "team player" or suggest you aren't willing to work hard. Even in our friendships, these pressures exist. We are expected to be present and engaged whenever our friends need us, responding with sympathy and agreeing to help in any way we can—which is a good thing, but these expectations can extend beyond our limits. For example, you may find you are struggling to afford the extensive plans and travel for your friend's wedding, but you worry if you try to tell her you need to work rather than attend every event, she may see you as uncaring or bring up the times she showed up for you.

No one wants to be thought of as a bad mom, a lazy colleague, or an uncaring friend. This, understandably, shapes your future approach to boundaries on your time and effort, because who wants to be viewed in such a negative light? Fear of these labels may cause you to juggle too many balls even though you're stretched so thin it's hard to enjoy the moment. You are also at risk of letting one of those balls fall, and then blaming yourself for getting it wrong.

What I want you to remember is that these expectations are unfair and biased. You haven't failed. Society has failed you. We exist in a patriarchal cultural framework alongside millions of other women around the world. Those who seek out my counsel cut across a wide range of professional and social strata. They're teachers and small-business owners, executives and stay-at-home moms, with a broad variety of interests, skills, and life goals. But they share a struggle with guilt and self-criticism, a common thread connecting them—and many of us. You, along with women everywhere, are responding in an understandable way to an inequitable system. You are being expected to carry far too much, with little support or understanding. Remember the Guilt Equation? Massive expectations lead to massive guilt, especially when we feel like we are falling short. We are being socialized to the point of exhaustion.

This may make you feel angry. It certainly has had that effect on me. Socialization causes so much suffering in the women I care for, in my friends and family, and certainly in me. We are tying ourselves into knots trying to reach that unattainable ideal and have been convinced it was all our idea. This is a truly powerful form of gaslighting. But that's what socialization has done to women.

Yet we are not powerless. We don't have to continue to buy into this rigged system. By illuminating the ugly influence of socialization on women's expectations, we can begin to regain our power. We can learn how to shift from "I just need to work harder to feel less guilt" to "Wow, these expectations are everywhere! No wonder I'm swimming in guilt." Not only will you spend less time criticizing your individual reactions, you will also begin to see yourself as part of something bigger.

Childhood Reinforcement

Socialization is initially reinforced and most strongly influenced by your closest relationships, particularly your earliest caretakers: your parents, grandparents, family members, and other caregivers. From birth, we look to them to learn about the world and our place in it.

Though your parents were, hopefully, trying their best, their decisions were shaped by the culture of the time, as well as their own upbringing and, yes, socialization. They learned their own versions of how a man or woman should behave in a particular role and passed these along to you. As you explored your world, they taught you about right and wrong and tried to help you reach their version of what they believed would be best for you. Sometimes, unfortunately, these lessons had unintended consequences, narrowing the path you viewed as possible or acceptable. Perhaps your mother had few opportunities to earn the stable income necessary to live independently, so she has always encouraged you to find a partner who could support you, emphasizing dating over career ambitions. So now you constantly criticize yourself for "failing" to meet someone special and spending too much time at work. Or maybe your father viewed his paternal role as one in which he should protect you from risk and disappointment, so he limited your freedom when you were younger. Now you take an avoidant approach to new people and experiences, feeling too scared to leave your comfort zone.

That said, some of this messaging wasn't always so direct or even intentional, but instead was absorbed as you navigated your unique childhood. Perhaps you were a people pleaser as a child because you recognized your younger siblings needed protection from a parent with anger issues, and keeping that parent calm was a responsibility you took on as the oldest sibling. Or maybe you learned to trust very few people after experiencing an early and painful loss, vowing to protect yourself from intimacy so you wouldn't be hurt again.

The ways you interpret your earliest interactions with the most important people in your life—including your family, friends, and romantic partners—are referred to in psychotherapy as *reflected appraisals*.[3] They can have lingering effects on your self-image. Picture a young girl tracing and cutting out a dress pattern in her size. Then, as she grows into an adult woman, she continues using the same design, believing it's the only possible option, even when it no longer applies. This can happen to you in your adult life, too. You may carry an unhelpful pattern—or expectation—for years, applying it in new situations and wondering why you can't find the right fit.

This is how these reflected appraisals can have long-standing negative—or at least limiting—influences on your self-perception and shape your expectations far into adulthood. Continuing to be a people pleaser may eventually lead to guilt because you bend over backward trying to make sure everyone is happy, inevitably failing because this is an impossible task. Avoiding intimacy to protect yourself from hurt might interfere with your ability to find and nurture a romantic relationship, something you really want. Or guilt may prevent you from pursuing an interest that doesn't align with the way your parents expect you to spend your time, because you view it as selfish to make decisions for your own happiness rather than to please them. Over time, you realize these fixed patterns are pushing you toward choices you no longer believe are best for you, as was the case with my client Nicole, a forty-four-year-old librarian.

Nicole grew up being told regularly to "keep it down," because her mother, an artist, was working in the back room and tended to become anxious and distracted when Nicole was making noise with her friends or during other activities. Nicole, an only child, described the guilt she would feel as a young girl when her mother told her she was being too loud and blamed her for migraine headaches: "I would tell myself I was an awful daughter, because I couldn't control myself." She eventually learned to play quietly alone and stopped inviting friends to visit. Her mother and others began to tell her she was a quiet, shy girl, and so this was how she learned to view herself.

Now Nicole is an adult in my office, struggling with feelings of boredom and restlessness at work and daydreaming about making a career change. However, this is causing guilt because she believes her mother would be disappointed by this desire.

"My mom is always talking about how similar we are," she

tells me. "She said if she hadn't become an artist, she would definitely be a librarian, like me."

It was hard for Nicole to explore her feelings, because even considering doing something else created guilt. "I should just be grateful to have a job. My mother always told me I could only depend on myself." As she begins to explore her recent experiences, however, she is surprised by what she discovers.

"I feel so energized at work when I'm speaking with our patrons," she says. "I love to hear about their interests and try to guide them to the best resources."

"Is that surprising to you?" I ask her.

"It is, actually!" she responds. "I always thought I was shy and didn't like to be around people, but maybe I'm actually an extrovert? That's wild! I've never really seen myself that way."

Reflected appraisals aren't always bad. Sometimes, they can help fortify your authentic desires. If you were repeatedly told by your parents that you should work in education because you were smart and caring, it might give you the confidence to pursue your dream of going to graduate school and help you survive the long nights of studying. However, as Nicole's story shows us, if the view your parents and others hold of you isn't aligned with your authentic gifts and desires, it will ultimately push you away from what you truly want.

Notice how reflected appraisals factor into the expectations you have about how you should behave in a particular role. How do you believe a woman "should" engage with her family? What would a "good daughter" do? What does it mean to be successful in your career? Is it possible to make a decision based on what you want, rather than what you perceive is the expected path? By carefully examining your childhood influences and how you may have adapted to your particular circumstances, you can begin to understand the seemingly unhelpful or unfair expectations you may hold for yourself today.

Changing World, Lingering Expectations

In addition to the powerful force that is socialization and its reinforcement in childhood, our expectations are shaped by another factor. As we learned in chapter 1, guilt comes up when you believe you have done something wrong. What you must also keep in mind, however, is that what is considered wrong for women is constantly in flux. In fact, you may be asked to be a different person in each of your many roles. Your supervisor expects you to be an assertive and engaged employee, taking on challenging projects while also being perpetually friendly and making sure your colleagues feel supported. You are asked to be a caring and calm mother who is also unnervingly organized and resourceful. In your romantic relationship, your partner may expect you to be relaxed and cheerful while also "keeping the mystery alive" with spontaneous, though well-planned, dates and thoughtful gifts. It just never ends.

Women have spent centuries overcoming the many ridiculous expectations and limitations placed on us solely because of our gender, either things we've been told we should do or those that society suggests we cannot do. We have pushed for and achieved massive change over the past one hundred years. Not terribly long ago, for example, it was considered wrong for women to vote, risking the "collapsing" of minds and bodies under the heavy weight of democratic participation.[4] It was also impossible for women in many fields to work while pregnant, or even if they were married. Many states in the early 1900s even banned married women from working as teachers, expecting them to instead focus on their home life and husband.

The barriers for women of color were even more extreme. Though the marriage ban may not have applied to those in housekeeping and other low-paying roles—roles held disproportionately by women of color—these women had no rights if they were unfairly paid or fired at the whim of their employers. And although women's right to vote was ratified in 1920, women of color still faced significant barriers to voting due to poll taxes, literacy tests, and other forms of disenfranchisement up to and even after the Voting Rights Act of 1965.

Fortunately, although barriers still exist to women's voting access, it is no longer illegal for women to cast a ballot, and we are now wielding increasingly influential power in many arenas. We can run for office, get our doctorate, buy a car, fly a plane. Indeed, we have overcome barrier after barrier to enter the many roles we hold in today's society. Name a profession and there are examples of rule breakers and pioneering women who have risked public shaming or worse by taking on challenges they were told a woman couldn't or shouldn't face. So in this way, it has been adaptive for us as women to push back on any attempts to limit our opportunities. We are leading companies, creating policy, making life-changing scientific breakthroughs, finding an increasingly receptive audience for our athletic power, and kicking ass all around the world.

However, in these modern circumstances, the choices made by our predecessors for their own survival—accepting their lack of equity in career choices or choosing marriage for financial security—are no longer serving the women of today. And unfortunately, society has struggled to keep pace with the changing landscape of women's lives. As a result, we are caught between the past and present in an increasingly exhausting way. Like many of us, you may have been raised being told you could be "anything you want to be." What this message left out, however, is that you would be expected to balance these new opportunities for the life you desired with all the caretaking duties and housework your predecessors were asked to complete. The old expectations haven't gone away. Instead, they've compounded.

Yes, now women can reach the highest echelons of academia, engage in public-facing leadership roles, nurture powerful careers, and choose our relationships based on love and connection rather than obligation and security, but not everything has changed. We are still expected to carry the disproportionate cognitive and emotional loads of childcare, household tasks, family schedules, and caretaking for our friends, colleagues, and loved ones, as well as to try to meet punishing beauty standards and face the constant encouragement to "improve" ourselves.

Because these unreachable—and conflicting—expectations have now compounded, we are forced to make very personal life decisions in a sea of judgment. Perhaps you have a thriving career and are repeatedly asked by your family and friends when you're going to "settle down and start a family," spending holidays and other social events defending your personal life from those who expect you to follow the traditional scripts. Alternatively, you may feel judged for deciding to stay home with your children rather than work outside the home, facing intrusive questions like "What, exactly, do you do all day?" and being expected to volunteer for every school event.

It doesn't matter if you are taking these paths out of necessity rather than choice. The incredibly high cost of childcare in this country might limit your ability to work in a job you enjoy because you actually lose money every month. Or you may be forced to work long hours to earn a living wage and don't have the time, energy, or opportunity to create the family you imagined. People will still judge. Self-criticism in the face of these realities just adds to your guilt and ignores the powerful forces working against you.

It also doesn't matter where you are in the world or how much social support you receive. Excessive guilt is a universal experience for women.

In a series of interviews, four women from Sweden, Germany, Italy, and the United States were asked about their experience of guilt. You might think women in the US—the only country of the four studied *without* broadly paid maternity leave or a minimum standard for sick or vacation days—would have the guiltiest women. The results of this research may surprise you.[5]

Let's start with Sweden, with its lengthy paid maternity and paternity leave and robust support for working parents in the form of state-funded, high-quality childcare. At 83 percent, Sweden has a very high percentage of women working, and three fourths of them are working full-time. Did this mom, when interviewed, describe any maternal guilt? Yep, quite a bit, actually. She discussed the guilt she felt every day if she didn't pick up her children early from daycare or didn't believe she had spent enough time with them. She also worried about which low-cost, high-quality daycare she should choose for her child, and described limiting time for herself or with friends in order to have enough energy for her career and her children. She regularly felt a large amount of guilt, especially on the days she believed she hadn't met her very high expectations.

How about in Germany? Fewer German women work outside the home, in part because of laws that encourage them to stay home early in their child's life, such as up to three years of maternity leave and few childcare options. If they do work, most are primary caregivers and as many as 70 percent of working women are in part-time jobs. The German woman interviewed in this case also described significant guilt, which in her case was related to working full-time. Though more women were starting to make this choice, she still felt she wasn't meeting the expectations of the ideal German woman, particularly in the amount of time and energy she could devote to her children. The norm was a part-time, flexible job, which allowed a mother to prioritize her children above all things. Not believing she met these high expectations, she described very frequent guilt.

Moving on to Italy, where women and men hold more traditional roles—the women primarily stay home to care for the children, while the men work. Compared with Sweden and Germany, a much lower percentage of mothers, only 55 percent, work outside the home. Childcare is very limited for children younger than age two, and women are required to take several months of maternity leave at 80 percent pay. The working mother interviewed described intense guilt that because of her full-time job, she was not living up to her expectations, set in part by her mother, who stayed home to care for her and her siblings. She worried she wasn't as connected to her children's lives as she perceived the nonworking mothers were. She also worried that her children saw her as a "stressed mom" because of her struggle to balance work and childcare, and that this was harmful for them. The guilt just kept piling on.

The American interviewed was notably distressed while she shared her concern about feeling like a "terrible mother." When asked to give advice to other women, she emphasized the inability to have a strong career, maintain a happy marriage, and be a good parent all at the same time. She believed she needed to constantly transition between trying to do well in these three roles and was never measuring up.

To summarize, though there were significant differences in paid maternity leave, childcare support, and cultural expectations of how much a mother should work outside the home, the women in all four countries described a nearly constant state of guilt. Their expectations were simply impossible to meet, particularly that they must always sacrifice their own needs for the good of their children.

We can't make broad judgments from these kinds of case studies, with a tiny sample size of just four women. This paper also represented only a fraction of the countries around the world that are filled with working mothers, and none of the women interviewed face the additional marginalization of racial or ethnic minorities. However, I share these stories here because they do suggest a concerning pattern: Women in each country were caught between societal expectations, slowly shifting cultural norms, and an unrelenting pressure to be all things to all people. This, understandably, burdened them with excessive and overwhelming guilt.

Expecting Less—and Living More

Recognizing you should no longer be expected to play *all* these roles is very different from being told, or telling yourself, that you *can't* do it all. You should have the right to choose what kind of woman you want to be, drawing from a wide variety of opportunities. No, you are not wrong to decide the most meaningful choice you can make is to stay home with your children. You are also allowed to recognize your life path will take you in a different direction, pouring effort and love into the creation of a meaningful career. Or maybe you want to do both, which is your absolute right. The important thing, regardless of the choice you make, is being wary of the expectations that inevitably come with each role and to let yourself be human. No one can do everything, all at once.

The problems do exist. There are too many things going on, too many responsibilities, too much to distract your attention, too many people in need. But this is not because you are personally failing. If you are to solve these problems, looking around to find someone to blame isn't always helpful, but it is particularly harmful when you repeatedly and critically blame yourself.

In physics, the law of conservation of matter teaches us that matter undergoing a reaction is neither created nor destroyed, but is instead *transformed.*[6] Trying to engage in the increasingly broad variety of roles open to women while simultaneously managing the household, performing constant caretaking, and keeping track of it all is simply impossible for just one person. Also because, unfortunately, you *cannot* create clones of yourself, you must leave behind the belief that every time you arrive at a barrier to continued growth, you should add to your already endless list of responsibilities. Instead, you must transform.

You can feel incredibly grateful for the choices women made long before you entered the world, under circumstances that called for their ingenuity and resilience, while still recognizing these exact choices may not be the best for you today. You can recognize you are being asked to take on an unsustainable number of roles in a culture stuck in the past, with expectations reflecting how things were rather than how they could be.

Adjusting your expectations may actually mean doing less. Not less living overall, but less ownership of all the tasks women previously held in different times. It might look like choosing a few evenings a week when another member of your family selects a dinner option, even if it's takeout, and you spend that time listening to a musician you love. It could be shifting your response at work from "Of course, I'm happy to do that" to "Let me take a look at my project load and get back to you." Can you imagine telling your most extroverted friend, "Actually, instead of going out for cocktails, what if we stayed in tonight and read books on the sofa together?"

By doing less in certain areas of your life, you open yourself up to more: more confidence pursuing your authentic path with agency, whether in a career or at home or both; more time for rest and regeneration; and more comfort relinquishing tasks that you no longer believe are the best use of your precious time. You might choose to start that crafting project shoved into your closet shelf or maybe have someone watch your kids while you take a walk or go to a movie alone. You could experience the relief of leaving the office with all your tasks done for the day because you've set reasonable limits on what you can achieve in eight hours. You may notice you are reaching out to friends more often because you know this might lead to activities you truly enjoy.

Yes, you may recognize disappointment or frustration in those around you if you start to say no to their constant demands or point out the impossibility of the current expectations. However, if you continue to pile on role after role, you will become depleted, left with only your own disappointment and guilt.

Importantly, it's not just your socialization that creates this expectation of omnipotence. Believing you are responsible does protect you from a different feeling that might show up in your life: helplessness. If you have to admit you cannot control the happiness of your children, the commitment of your spouse, the fluctuating job market, or the health of your parents, this can trigger painful feelings of anxiety and disappointment. The guilt of responsibility, then, at least means you feel like you can *do* something about the pain.

To move beyond excessive guilt, you must begin to accept that the cost of your ability to love and grow is the vulnerability of an uncertain future, both for you and for the important people in your life. The only way to truly prevent loss is to sacrifice the joy that comes with deep and intimate connection and awareness. Learning to live with imperfection and uncertainty, though it can feel incredibly unsettling, will actually open you to a new horizon of meaning, engagement, and joy in your precious life.

※

As you finish this chapter, you are now able to recognize the socialization at the heart of your experience with excessive guilt. You understand how you have been taught, both by broader society and by members of your most intimate circle, to play the role of the Ideal Woman. Times have indeed changed, and women are pushing hard against any limitations placed in our path, but we are still not free of the long-standing, unfair, and often unreachable standards placed on us by those who benefit from our exhaustive efforts. Remember, according to the Guilt Equation, sky-high expectations, whether from ourselves or others, are a recipe for intense guilt. In this next chapter, you will learn about four of the most pervasive, unhelpful, and draining types of expectations we face as modern women. I call them the *Four Furies*, and they are everywhere.

The Four Furies of Unreasonable Expectations

The unrealistic and unhelpful expectations women are socialized to have, overwhelming us with painful guilt, can be boiled down to four types. I call them the Four Furies: Constant Caretaking, Hyper-Accountability, Seeking Perfection, and Trying to Have It All.

If you take a close look at the underlying expectations driving your sense of guilt, you'll likely find one of these at their core. It's not just you, and it's not just me. It's all of us. As you start recognizing these common triggers, you may have a mix of emotions, including sadness and grief, because you've lived with their draining effects for so long. That's understandable. The reason it's still so important to learn about them, though, is because you can't push back on a shadow. Bringing these expectations into the light, they can be named, understood, and ultimately drained of their power over your life.

Therefore, let's explore each of these in detail, so you will get a crystal-clear understanding of the pressures you face, and you'll feel empowered to move beyond their limiting effects.

Constant Caretaking: I Should Take Care of Others Before Myself (Even at My Own Expense)

Women are expected to be caretakers for family members, friends, even colleagues. We are disproportionately expected to prioritize the needs and desires of others, even when they conflict with our own needs. When you were young, you might have been asked to babysit for your siblings or young cousins or allow them to tag along when you left the house. You might have been tasked with caring for an elderly loved one because your parents were at work. These caregiving roles grow alongside us, showing up in each phase of our lives to create unhelpful and unreachable expectations. You stay up late to comfort a friend going through a difficult breakup, even though you have an exam the next day. You cancel a key meeting because your child has a fever and needs to come home from school, and your husband says he can't leave work.

Guilt creeps up when we behave in a way that's contradictory to caretaking—like when you consider telling your friend you're too exhausted from a long workweek to attend her birthday party. In these moments, guilt pushes you to override your own needs so you won't risk letting others down.

You may see yourself as a compassionate person and want to help others, but when you relentlessly prioritize the needs, wishes, and health of everyone else, you grow increasingly depleted in the process. In addition, because perfection in these roles is not possible, you often believe you have failed in some way, and your guilt intensifies. This creates a difficult cycle of striving to do everything for your loved ones, while you feel increasingly drained.

Responding to any limits on your caretaking with intense guilt also leads to an unwanted shift of responsibilities over time. For example, maybe you have noticed your husband, previously a fairly neat and organized bachelor, is no longer helping you keep the house clean and tends to leave his things everywhere. You, then, spend evenings after work cleaning up, feeling frustrated and unclear about how this happened. This is how this polarization of function occurs, and it certainly isn't limited to romantic relationships. You take on more and more tasks as a friend, employee, volunteer, or in one of your many other roles, while your loved one or colleague takes a step back, maybe to rebalance the relationship, or perhaps they're just happy to relinquish these less-than-desirable tasks. Once these roles become fixed, it creates a difficult cycle. You do more, they do less, you add to your expectations, and they think everything is working out quite well, thank you very much.

Yes, your loved ones, friends, even colleagues may view you as increasingly competent and efficient, which may feel good at first. But notice how this creates expectations you find difficult to shed. You may be hesitant to relinquish this image of yourself as a caring, thoughtful superwoman, so you just keep stepping it up one more notch, until you're at the edge of a cliff, forced into a monumental choice between perfect caretaking and utter selfishness. In addition, rather than recognizing these expectations are unfair and unbalanced, you may struggle with a constant state of resentment toward others while also berating yourself for feeling overwhelmed.

I wish the people in your life would recognize this imbalance and jump in to help you, but, like far too many of us, you may end up sitting alone late at night, staring at your endless to-do list and trying to identify every possible tool within yourself to overcome, or at least cope with, an overwhelming number of responsibilities. Organization! Time-management training! Color-coded calendars! Yoga to clear the mind! Journaling! But these are just Band-Aids over a much bigger problem.

Without addressing the bigger problem—these outsized

expectations—things can get pretty dark. By repeatedly suppressing our own needs as we prioritize others', we are absorbing a powerful, painful message: I don't matter. From here, we don't have far to travel toward very negative outcomes. You may notice an increase in harsh self-criticism, avoidance via binge eating, drinking too much, or compulsive shopping, even just keeping so damn busy you don't leave any room for thoughts. These strategies further increase your guilt, you end up feeling even worse, and the days just keep rolling by.

What if, instead of viewing it as some sort of weakness, prioritizing our own needs and desires was seen as a logical and recommended approach? Can you imagine a world where inviting others to take part in problem-solving actually meant you were empowered, innovative, and wise? What if society praised you for admitting, "I am not always in control," and rewarded you for your ability to seek support, rally community, and ask for help? Also, importantly, what if you were allowed to have some downtime whenever it made sense for you? Can you imagine resting even when the emails haven't been answered, there are dishes in the sink, or your child wants to show you their latest work of art?

Unfortunately, this will not change in broader society until we begin to make a shift internally—not because it's our fault, but because we are only truly able to change ourselves. However, this shift is possible. Can you imagine living in a future where your needs are also considered? You would recognize the signs of a stressful day, and instead of burying them in tasks to help everyone else's lives run more smoothly, you would take an hour to sit quietly in your favorite chair while you listened to music you love. You would choose tasks in the office that you viewed as a meaningful contribution to society, rather than agreeing to plan an office party no one else was willing to take on. You would turn your well-honed, powerful caregiving skills back to yourself, making sure your body was well fed, your sleep was long and restorative, and your mood was supported by enjoyable activities. In other words, you would make sure your needs were actually met. It could create a significant change and begin to lower all this miserable, draining guilt.

Let's look at some of the most common areas where this constant caretaking expectation rears its ugly head.

The Perfect Mother

> "If I were a better mom, my kids would
> never feel sad or disappointed."

Sarah, a forty-four-year-old married orthodontist, was briefly in tears as she described an interaction with her daughter from earlier in the week, shaking her head in frustration about its lingering effects.

"I keep replaying the decisions leading up to that day and

feeling so guilty that I didn't remember to take that time off for her school concert! I'm such a terrible mom."

Guilt can take so many forms for women: about our diet adherence, exercise frequency, career mobility, disconnection from friends or family, or lack of community engagement. However, some of the most intense experiences of guilt emerge in our role as a parent. Indeed, at the heart of society's expectations for women is our role as the primary caretaker in the family home, with a selfless offering of nurturing, dedication, and sacrifice preached everywhere from custom T-shirts to cleaning supply commercials. From your earliest years, you have been socialized to put the needs of others before your own—and this culminates in no more forceful, more overwhelming way than in motherhood. Whether you become a mother through pregnancy, adoption, or other means, the pressure to be a perfect mom is relentless.

From my seat, I could see all the ways that Sarah was a great mother. She cared deeply for her daughter and son, frequently mentioning the thoughtful conversations they had together. But if she were to describe her own Guilt Equation, she would just see her failure to meet her sky-high caretaking expectations.

Remember, guilt increases the further our reality departs from our expectations; that is, what we believe should happen. As mothers, we have expectations of constant care and vigilance. We are expected to protect our children from disappointment, sadness, and loneliness and anticipate their every need and desire. We are judged harshly if we cannot provide constant screen-free entertainment, healthy homemade dinners, and endless enrichment opportunities, all while projecting the unfazed, organized, and loving image of the perfect mother. Guilt can even become a type of reassurance, confirming your love, but it has a high cost. You may create an unsustainable pattern of responding to feelings of guilt with excessive gifts of your time and effort. The guilt then leads to building resentment and drains you of the very energy you need to live your life, whether that involves spending time with your kids, reading a great book, or meeting a friend at the park for a nap under a giant oak tree.

In the past month, have you thought, like Sarah, "I'm a terrible mom"? If the answer is yes, you are certainly not alone. As Sarah and I began to explore the content of her self-talk, she realized she was constantly criticizing her efforts and setting unfair expectations of being the perfect mother. She noticed common toxic thoughts such as "I'm doing a bad job raising my kids," which understandably triggered feelings of sadness, guilt, and disappointment. I asked Sarah to share some of her other recent guilty thoughts; see if you can relate:

"I should be at every event and volunteer for school activities, even when I'm overwhelmed at work."

"I should make sure my son never has trouble at school, so I can guarantee his future at a good college."

"If I were a better mom, I would never yell at my kids."

Think about your typical experience of parental guilt. Do you notice a pattern of holding yourself to incredibly high expectations as a mother, which you can't realistically meet? Maybe you tell yourself a good mother would never forget something important in her child's life, like a school concert, or take time for herself despite laundry piling up. She would enjoy every moment of motherhood and embrace the constant sacrifices required of her in this role, per society's version of the perfect mother.

The way we combat guilt in motherhood is by lowering our expectations and acknowledging the things we're already doing well. In other words, by embracing our humanity—and humans are not perfect. In psychology, pediatrician and psychoanalyst D. W. Winnicott coined the phrase "good enough mother."[1] Adapted to her baby's needs, the good enough mother allows her children to experience some frustration as they encounter the outside world. Consider what it might feel like to shift your expectations for yourself from perfection to good enough. Instead of saying yes to pushing your child on the swing for another hour, even though you're tired or annoyed, you say no and let your child be disappointed—but you get the break you need. Though a challenging balancing act, this approach to parenting can provide kids room for building confidence and exploring independently. In fact, saying no to their request on the swings might prompt your child to walk up to a new friend and ask them to play. To state it plainly, you *do not* need to be perfect to raise happy, well-adjusted kids. By setting fair expectations while noticing the moments you do authentically enjoy, you can find a way to move forward with love and intention, rather than excessive and energy-sapping guilt.

Why Holidays Can Be So Difficult

Holidays are likely a time when your attempt to take care of everyone goes into overdrive. Expectations for a particular event are often a combination of powerful cultural and religious traditions, challenging family dynamics, and pressure to perform according to an unreachable ideal.

You may take pleasure in traditions such as gift-giving and special recipes, but when it comes to holidays, turning yourself inside out to get everything right, with the goal of creating only the most joyful memories possible for everyone, creates an enormous burden of unrealistic expectations.

Also, none of us can hide how the busy holiday season affects us. Your loved ones might see a tired, frustrated woman trying to get everything right while she misses the fun herself.

Now, when you think back to your own experiences, watch out for a critical response, such as "You're right. I need to make sure I'm happier and more cheerful during the holidays." This is not what it means to set fair expectations, but rather reflects a continuation of you taking on responsibility for absolutely everything.

What if, instead, you started from the goal of how you want to feel during the holiday season? Maybe your dream is to feel the warmth and connection of a particular tradition, or to create your own simple moments, but you worry this wouldn't be "fun or exciting enough" for your loved ones. However, in this situation, consider what your loved ones might feel when they empathize with you. Would they feel anxious, tired, frustrated, and overwhelmed? Or rather, calm, happy, and engaged? If these latter feelings are the goal, how can you work backward to imagine the holiday preparations and events with this in mind? What would it take for you to reach the big day with something other than exhaustion and dread?

It may mean you must find a way to do less. Maybe your exhaustive efforts aren't necessary to create an atmosphere of connection and tradition. Maybe you can slow way down, such as planning to cut the special recipes down to something simple but delicious, placing a limit on gift-giving in your family so you aren't chasing the elusive "enough," and making sure you have time to rest, even if it means declining a party invitation to watch old movies or take a walk to clear your head.

Can you possibly approach the holidays with more reasonable expectations? You will need to remember you are not responsible for the feelings of others, even when you really love them and want so much for them to have a magical experience. You must also live with the lack of control you have over the events other people remember and enjoy. Instead, imagine what it would look like to present a very human and loving woman who knows things will go wrong and feelings will be mixed, but you show up anyway, hoping for the best and letting go of perfection.

The Perfect Daughter

"I should choose the career, partner, or life path my parents expect, because otherwise I'm ungrateful."

The perfect daughter is expected to always anticipate the needs and wishes of her parents, respond lovingly and patiently, and skillfully accept their advice while also protecting them from feeling overwhelmed by her challenges or difficult decisions. She must be available, cheerful, and unfazed by criticism at all times, and know how to support her parents without undermining their sense of independence. In other words, she must be superhuman.

As a teenager, you probably pushed limits, seeking independence from your parents, relying more on peers as well as other adults—such as coaches and teachers—to guide your decisions and behavior. You may now look back on this time as a period of rebellion in which you made somewhat questionable choices and learned important lessons the hard way. However, you needed this push and pull to help you figure out who you were meant to be. One of the challenges of daughterhood, at any age, is that we are still in this process of push and pull. Even if you continue to have a very close relationship with your parents, conflict is inevitable because, as an adult, you are able to make your own decisions based on your own values and goals. You may share many of these with your parents, but rarely all of them—which is absolutely normal.

Setting unrealistic expectations of caretaking in daughterhood can lead to guilt and resentment. You may view the perfect daughter as one who demonstrates gratitude for her parents' care and support, which is inherently a good thing. However, by believing you must demonstrate this gratitude through constant sacrifice, such as turning down an exciting job promotion in another city so you won't miss regular family dinners, you are letting guilt push you away from your own wishes and desires.

What scripts are you following for what a perfect daughter would do? Where did these expectations arise? Maybe your parents lived near their parents and you always expected to do so, too. Perhaps several generations of your relatives worked in the same family-owned business, but your dream is to become an artist. If your expectation is that the perfect daughter would never make choices that would upset her family, you are in a difficult bind and guaranteed to feel guilt and disappointment.

Major life transitions are often when our expectations of perfect daughterhood come to a head with reality and create considerable conflict within families. One of the reasons these times can be so fraught is because you each carry the powerful cultural traditions of those who came before you. For example, think of all the opportunities for expectations a typical wedding creates. You are attempting to merge two distinct families, each with their own traditions and expectations, while also forging a new life with another, unique person. Maybe you decide to plan a small destination wedding rather than being married in your family's church, which greatly disappoints your parents, who are expecting a similar service to their own, many years ago. If you are close with them and believe a good daughter would never hurt her parents, the guilt can be overwhelming.

Another example: becoming a parent. When you bring home a new baby, every decision can seem momentous, from what to name this new family member to sleep-training and feeding decisions, even what kind of toys you choose for them. Your well-meaning parents remember the choices they made and, look, you turned out all right, didn't you? Why not just do it the way they did? If your expectation is to be a daughter who always listens to her elders and tries to avoid conflict or differences of opinion, parenthood will be a minefield. You are caring for this new, helpless creature, while also trying to manage your parents' expectations. Wouldn't a good daughter let her mother hold the baby while she does housework? It makes your mother so happy. So what if you're exhausted and would absolutely love some help with a meal or two, or even prefer to take a nap with the baby while someone miraculously cleans up the kitchen? The perfect daughter always says yes.

The process of caretaking for aging parents and grandparents can be particularly guilt-inducing. If they are beginning to rely on you for more of their personal needs, you are forced into a parenting role with them, sometimes even as you parent your own children. In these situations, based on expectations of ideal caretaking, you may often feel like you're not doing enough.

Maybe your mother took in her mother-in-law when she was elderly and frail, and now you feel terrible for making a different decision, believing your home couldn't safely accommodate twenty-four-hour care for a parent.

What makes caring for aging family members even harder is that you cannot expect progress toward independence and maturity. You are forced to adjust your expectations for them, while caring for them in new and difficult ways, even as you grieve the loss of the people they used to be and the important roles they played in your life. Reacting to these painful changes, you might set caretaking expectations for yourself that are even more impossible to meet. You might vow to visit your ailing father every day, even if this strains your ability to complete work projects or means missing key moments in your spouse's or children's lives. You might spend all your time with your mother, suggesting activities she could do at the local community center or lining up a therapist for her, and feel disappointed and frustrated when she doesn't follow through or doesn't seem to be feeling any better. Maybe you stop sharing challenges in your own life to protect your parents from worry, removing one of your most helpful outlets for support and encouragement.

It's difficult to separate the choices you make from those your parents made or would prefer you make, and they may view your departure from their path as some kind of rejection. This can be so painful. Most of us still want to please our parents and express gratitude for their love and care over the years. What kind of daughter rejects her parents' helpful advice? You can see how your expectations can keep you trapped in an endless loop of trying to please everyone—and losing yourself in the process.

Imagine what it might look like to be a "good enough" daughter. Rather than seeking perfection, could you consider something more attainable? It's important to remember, at the core of your constant efforts to protect your parents from disappointment and sadness is your deep and abiding love. This can be highlighted in ways that don't create self-deprivation and resentment, but rather open communication for a balanced relationship. Maybe you've chosen a career path that doesn't align with their childhood expectations of you, becoming a professional musician rather than a lawyer, for example. Could you point out the aspects of your pursuit, including determination, persistence, and creativity, that would bridge these two options, reminding your parents of the positive legacy they've created, while also limiting your self-flagellation for letting them down? Could you focus your conversations on subjects where you can find some common ground, and try to foster connection without capitulation? Your guilt may lessen if you focus on the love and gratitude you feel for your parents, even though they are also imperfect human beings who likely tried their best, made choices aligned with their values, and love you no matter what.

The Perfect Partner

"A good partner would make sure her decisions never
interfered with her loved one's happiness."

In our romantic relationships, our socialization as caregivers
may mean we bend over backward trying to become the person
we believe our partners want or need us to be, rather than who
we actually are. This is especially so for women, who are socialized to be responsible for the health of a relationship. You
may be afraid to share your own needs or concerns, because it
could have a negative effect on your partner. Maybe you believe
the ideal girlfriend would always be willing to participate in
the same activities as her partner, and you feel guilty when this
expectation is challenged by their love of camping, something
you would prefer to only read about in mystery novels. Or you
expect yourself to be in a good mood every evening because you
want your spouse to feel loved, and a good wife would find a
way to overcome her own stress and just be cheerful.

Suppressing your own feelings and desires, however, interferes with closeness and creates a lopsided support structure,
serving no one. You cannot mother your partner, nor should
you strive to do so. In a truly healthy and loving relationship,
you and your partner will take care of each other equally,
though your individual needs may ebb and flow. Also, although
you may know your loved one very well, you cannot perfectly

predict how they will perceive or respond to a particular situation, and in the attempt to be the perfect partner, you might make unfair assumptions. Remember, no one can prevent you from the experience of negative emotions, no matter how intensely they care for you, and you can love someone with every cell in your body but still be unable to prevent them from feeling sadness or grief. To expect this of yourself or others just leads to disappointment and dissatisfaction.

What's more, trying to be the perfect partner often results in projecting those outsize expectations onto them, further heightening your feelings of guilt. You may feel disappointed, for example, because you've planned an elaborate date night and your spouse doesn't seem excited to be there. If you're carrying the unfair expectation that your effort is only worthwhile if he responds in a particular way—which is out of your control—you can feel guilty even when you've tried your best. Sure, a bad date night is disappointing, but what if that didn't mean you were a "bad" spouse but, instead, was seen as an opportunity to learn from each other? For example, you may love trying a new, critically acclaimed restaurant, while he would prefer grabbing some popcorn and heading to a movie. The key here is recognizing how expectations of perfect romantic connection are actually contributing to your guilt, and knowing there can be another way.

Although romantic comedies suggest we will finally find

"the one" and fit perfectly like two puzzle pieces, the true story is something more complex. Rather than seeking perfection, each individual in a relationship needs to build empathy toward the other and recognize when they are viewing a different childhood blueprint. The caretaking must be a mutual effort, with the goal of both individuals becoming their best selves. Remember, your reflected appraisals are not fixed images, and they can be adjusted to better meet current needs, though this takes time, patience, and a willingness to look inward and communicate clearly.

Hyper-Accountability: I Can and Should Control Others' Feelings

Have you ever caught yourself trying to control someone else's feelings, believing they were your responsibility? Perhaps you deep-cleaned your home for a week before your mother arrived, so she wouldn't be disappointed. Or you spent a ridiculous amount of money on your son's eighth birthday party because you wanted to "make sure" he was happy.

As a human, your ability to empathize means you are skilled at recognizing, even experiencing, the way someone else is feeling. You can see when someone is in pain or feeling frightened, frustrated, or disappointed, and this awareness can help guide your approach to that individual. As you learned earlier, children as young as three can already demonstrate empathic skills, which are part of our highly successful adaptations as a social species.

However—and this is key—just because you can skillfully interpret the way people are feeling doesn't mean you can control those feelings. Nor should you hold yourself accountable for their emotions, because when you do, you blame yourself if the desired outcome is not reached. You may believe you should be able to improve your friend's mood when she is having a difficult day or remove a loved one's disappointment over a painful setback. When they continue to have these difficult emotions despite your efforts, you might feel like a failure. This, then, can contribute to a constant feeling of falling behind or not doing enough—and there it is again: guilt.

From a young age, women are highly socialized to pay careful attention to others' emotions, allowing us to be responsive caregivers. Although truly controlling someone else's emotions is impossible, that doesn't mean you haven't been repeatedly asked to take responsibility for those feelings. Maybe as a teenager you were told by your father, "Your mom seems pretty down today. You should really try to cheer her up," or you were asked to keep exciting news quiet so you wouldn't upset a sibling who was having a difficult day. When you are told over and over again to monitor the experiences of others, adjust your own behaviors to make sure others are feeling good, and accept responsibility any time your loved ones are in pain, of course you're going to try to meet these expectations. Why?

First, because it often feels good to see yourself as the kind of caring, thoughtful person who would make these choices to help others. Also, the sense of control it creates can foster hope in the face of another person's pain, because perhaps you can fix it—though, of course, you can't. Lastly, believing you've disappointed others is an awful feeling, and you may try to do whatever you can to avoid that experience, even if it means taking on the impossible task of trying to control someone else's feelings.

How does this attempt to control others' emotions show up in your day-to-day life? You double down on your attempts to control *everything*. You over-function, with a frantic accumulation of tasks, worries, and expectations that leave you feeling even more overwhelmed while also giving you the illusion of being in control. Eventually, you take on so much, you begin to feel accountable for the comfort and happiness of every single person you encounter.

This pattern shows up over and over in my therapy sessions. My clients are strong, assertive women who create and attain ambitious goals for themselves but feel flummoxed by the disproportionate roles they play in completing household tasks or office administrative duties. I imagine you, like many of them, can describe in detail the cognitive load you carry each day, made up of the numerous appointments, responsibilities, and needs you track for everyone else.

But at the root of this is fear: fear that someone is going to suffer because of something you did or didn't do. Just ask yourself, what would happen if you relinquished some of these tasks? Do you immediately think about who would feel disappointed or who might miss an important activity or appointment that might affect them negatively? Your first thought is how *others* might feel, like the coach if your child missed a soccer practice, your colleagues if the office kitchen was noticeably messier than usual, or the vet if you haven't remembered to give your dog his heartworm medicine for way too long.

Now, rather than accusing yourself of getting this wrong, let's acknowledge how powerfully you were socialized to respond to this threat of upsetting others by taking on all responsibility. Choosing a different approach requires a break from the repeated messages you've absorbed since childhood: Girls must be responsible, caring people, sensitive to the feelings of others, and they must do their best to help others feel better. If someone feels bad and you care about that person, you should try to do something, right? Even if you don't actually have the power to truly change their emotions? Otherwise, do you really care?

The answer is yes. You care very, very much. You just recognize you cannot control the thoughts and feelings of others, even when you really want to. Even if you are willing to add just one more thing to your list of daily tasks.

Though it may take some mental gymnastics, women are amazingly creative in finding ways to hold themselves accountable for the experiences of others. You might feel guilty when your friend tells you she's lonely and really wants to find a romantic partner, because you think if you were a better friend, you would have found someone for her or at least cheered her up with fun activities. Maybe you scramble to plan a special dinner for your son, because he's upset about something at school and you believe it's your job as a mother to immediately reverse his low mood.

However, you must learn how to help those you love *without* taking responsibility for their pain. Shift from telling yourself, "I'm such a bad friend, letting her feel this way," to saying, "This is really hard. I wish I could help her find love, but I can just try to be there when she needs to talk." From thinking, "If I'm a good mom, my son should never feel sad," to "Of course he's going to have these feelings. I can't fix it, but I can be there for him and show him love and support."

Remember, no matter how hard you work, how diligently you keep track, or how self-sacrificing you become, you cannot control the thoughts and emotions of other people. Therefore, you are set up to fail. Like a carnival game, carrying responsibility for things outside your control forces you to try over and over against a rigged system, sure that each attempt you make will finally win you that giant stuffed panda. This is why this type of expectation is so difficult. Not only does it push you to take on far too much, it also can make you feel like a constant failure, letting others down.

Remember, no one has this kind of omnipotence or succeeds at everything all the time. Our attempts to do so make sense, however, when we consider the next major expectation women face: the expectation to be perfect.

Seeking Perfection: With Enough Self-Control, I Can Be Perfect

If men are rewarded for assertive control over the greater world, women seem to be rewarded—through love, attention, praise, and idealization—for maintaining self-control. This manifests in countless ways. You've probably felt a pressure to have control over your body, your home, the health and happiness of your family, your emotions, your biological aging, your intensity, your ambition, your calendar, your thoughts, and on and on and on. This self-control, you're told, will allow you to live up to society's expectation (which often becomes your own):

perfection. From a very young age, you have been socialized to believe this is what you must achieve to be worthy of love and attention.

Research suggests perfectionism—the combination of exceedingly high standards and highly critical self-assessment[2]—has been increasing in recent decades and can elevate risks of hopelessness, depression, and anxiety.[3] The reasons for this are complex, but some key factors exist. For example, in a globally connected world, we have unparalleled awareness of people who are at the top of their field, setting standards that are at an unreachable level. We see a famous musician or professional athlete and assume they are magically superior to us in all aspects of their lives. This assumption, which ignores the reality of their likely setbacks, exhausting hours of practice, and numerous sacrifices to reach near-perfection in just this one area, is not only inaccurate but can also feel highly demoralizing.

Social media, a veritable comparison machine, puts endless images of filtered perfection in your face whenever you scroll, elevating expectations to a sky-high level. Also, women in particular are subject to the high standards and critical self-assessment of perfectionism, thanks to the perpetuation of very narrow definitions of beauty and optimal body types, an unfair tendency to be labeled negatively for traits that might be reason for praise in men, such as assertiveness or ambition, and the perception—and often the reality—of limited spots for women at the top of their fields, creating pressure to be infallible in all things if we want a fighting chance at success.

This increasingly common pursuit of perfection is not making our lives better. In fact, a specific version called *socially prescribed perfectionism* is particularly problematic.

Socially prescribed perfectionism is the perception that very high expectations are coming from others, rather than yourself. Instead of needing to be perfect because you feel it's the "right" thing to do, you feel you need to be perfect because otherwise you will not be valued or accepted by others. For example, you believe a romantic partner will only be attracted to you if you're at your very best, in full makeup, hair blown out, and wearing sexy lingerie. Or at the gym, you may worry that other people are judging your muscle tone and endurance, expecting you to be some kind of fitness queen. At work, you might cringe if your report has a typo or you forget to cc your manager on an important email, assuming everyone will think you're a mess because you aren't perfectly organized and efficient.

This type of perfectionism can not only worsen your self-esteem, it can also markedly increase feelings of demoralization—the experience of feeling helpless or hopeless because you think you lack the skills necessary to cope with a particular situation.[4] Interestingly, one study even demonstrated that socially prescribed perfectionism was more likely to lead to demoralization than recent negative life events, such as failing an academic course, being involved in a minor car accident, even breaking up with a romantic partner.[5] That is quite a toxic effect!

Socially prescribed perfectionism not only creates unreachable expectations and the resulting guilt, but can also cause you to believe you've let *others* down, which causes you to fear that they might pull away from you. The threat of losing this crucial social support can be particularly painful, especially if you think it's your own fault. To make matters worse, socially prescribed perfectionism doesn't typically trigger support from your loved ones, because the pain it creates can be invisible. In fact, members of your support network may actually be more likely to praise your attempts to reach perfection ("Wow, you never miss a workout, even when you're sick!"), pushing you further toward unreasonable goals. Additionally, you might not be aware of your perfectionistic approaches, only noticing the ways you've fallen short. You tell yourself you're lazy after missing one day at the gym or you call yourself a failure because your productivity dipped slightly last month in the face of a prolonged flu or a major change in responsibilities.

Truly, perfectionism, especially the socially prescribed type, is likely doing you quite a bit of harm. It's causing your guilt to skyrocket far beyond helpful levels, and burdening you with unreasonable expectations of self-control and self-improvement.

It is also interfering with your ability to create and maintain crucial social support. Having the "best" body or being the "best" mother or the "best" employee suggests that if you just continue to take on more tasks and responsibilities—while striving for perfect self-improvement—you can "win" in these roles. But this is truly a fool's errand. There's no such thing as perfect. Relentlessly seeking a better version of yourself just sets you up to constantly feel guilty for falling short of these idealized expectations.

Let's dig a little deeper into areas where this expectation of perfection can lead to toxic guilt.

The Perfect Body

"If I could just lose ten pounds,
I might start dating again."

Few aspects of our lives create more self-critical thoughts and unrealistic, harmful expectations than those around our bodies. According to current societal standards, a woman's perfect body might be described as lighter skinned, able-bodied, thin, and fit, yet somehow also optimally curvy, though these characteristics are constantly changing, leaving us scrambling to adjust.

Like so many women, you may spend enormous amounts of time seeking out ways to lose weight and improve or hide unwanted aspects of your appearance. As early as elementary school, girls describe actively dieting to lose weight, and they discuss their bodies in very negative terms. They also begin describing guilt for choices they have made in their food intake and activities—guilt that carries into adulthood. Even if you are generally satisfied with your body, you may still notice unrealistic expectations you set for yourself, such as believing you should always be dressed fashionably or never allowing yourself to appear tired or ill, even when you may be fighting off a terrible cold or coping with significant menstrual cramps. You may also be setting your standards for fitness at unachievable heights, based on comparisons with women you see as ideal in your life as well as on television or social media. This causes you to feel constantly undesirable or out of shape, and encourages you to overlook the many ways your body is healthy, strong, and beautiful.

The expectations created by society's tendency to stigmatize any body that doesn't conform to these ideals are doing you real harm. After all, since as early as you can recall, powerful socialization has taught you to judge those in imperfect bodies as lacking willpower and representing unhealthy habits, or as undesirable people, at risk of rejection. The judgments you make about yourself are difficult to shift in a culture that prizes an incredibly limited variety of bodies. You didn't just make this stuff up.

Your socialization to be hyper-responsible also shows up in your quest for the perfect body. If you perceive that others are judging you for your appearance or believe you're not reaching the perfect size or shape, you may experience significant guilt, believing you have done something wrong. The guilt and shame that follow these critical messages about your body then become barriers to body acceptance, positive self-talk, and motivation to make healthy choices.

This is important. Self-criticism is *not* motivating. In fact, true motivation actually occurs when we take the opposite approach.[6] In the coming chapters, you will learn about the power of self-compassion to help you overcome these unrealistic comparisons and harsh criticism—from others as well as yourself—and begin working toward acceptance.

Perfect Mental Health

"Why can't I stop feeling so anxious all the time? Other people seem to cope better with their stress."

In addition to expectations around our bodies and appearance, women also feel pressure to maintain perfect mental health. If you have experienced anxiety, depression, or other mental health concerns, you may notice you are trying to cope with these challenges in some idealized way, such as practicing daily meditation or eating an anti-inflammatory diet, rather than "depending on" evidence-based treatments like therapy or medication. I'm not saying meditation and a healthy diet are bad, but creating unfair expectations about how you are "supposed" to find relief leads to demoralization, and it can exacerbate your already painful anxiety or depression.

Repeatedly telling yourself you are falling short when you don't measure up to sky-high expectations of mental "wellness" just makes you feel that much worse. You may expect yourself to sail through that job interview with zero anxiety or recover from a painful loss without periods of intense sadness. In fact, if you expect to be able to "just snap out of it," recognizing and seeking appropriate treatment, if it even occurs, can carry the burden of failure, causing you to feel even more guilty. You might accuse yourself of being weak if you need to take some time off to heal, or you may believe others will assume you're totally irresponsible or crazy if you have to leave a class or meeting due to a panic attack or if you begin taking medication or working with a therapist.

Lowering guilt about symptoms of anxiety, depression, or other mental health challenges involves lowering your expectation of perfect health. As with most species, our brains are designed to respond to our environment. However, unique to humans, you can create sophisticated narratives about your past experiences and anticipate possible risks in the future. When, through a combination of genetics, environment, and experiences, these sophisticated functions become disrupted, you can get caught in painful regrets about prior choices or overwhelmed by intrusive, anxious thoughts.

In addition to helping you recognize your own unfair expectations, addressing stigma about mental illness will hopefully shift the culture of personal responsibility to a more realistic, scientifically accurate understanding of symptoms. You are no more able to "just cheer up" when you are depressed than you are to "just start walking" with a broken leg. The truth is, most of us will have periods in our lives when we are struggling with some aspect of our mental health, from panic attacks to depression to heightened anxiety. Setting unrealistic expectations of perfection in this area can add unnecessary burdens to your life, and you deserve compassion, rather than criticism, as you try to cope.

The Perfect Sexual Being

> "I should be more excited to have sex,
> even if it doesn't always feel that great."

Sexual guilt deserves its own book. So many women describe ways guilt can interfere with satisfying intimacy. Maybe you've experienced a mismatch in sexual desire compared to your partner or you've noticed how insecurities about your body create barriers to intimacy. Sex can be a minefield for unhelpful expectations and self-criticism, particularly for women.

Striving for perfection in this area, as in many others we've discussed, can cause you to experience excessive guilt and self-criticism. You are not a machine, and your desire and arousal are not buttons that someone can push for an automatic response. Expecting this of yourself is a recipe for misery and guilt. Also, not surprisingly, believing others—particularly your partner—expect you to be perfect can exacerbate this guilt.[7] Not only can this type of perfectionism increase your sexual anxiety and decrease your sexual self-esteem, it can also diminish your desire and arousal, particularly lubrication, which can actually lead to sexual pain and make it more difficult for you to reach orgasm. All in all, believing that your partner expects you to be a superstar in bed can put a major damper on your sexual enjoyment.

Many of us are overlooking the multiple important ways we are helping to create intimacy with our partner. Maybe you didn't spend the entire day covering your bedroom in rose petals and shopping for high-end lingerie. That doesn't mean you aren't giving your partner your time, attention, and willingness to have fun, making space in your very busy life to connect with them. This is a powerful and generous thing.

Aging Perfectly

**"I know I'm supposed to enjoy the freedom
of retirement, but why do I feel so lost?"**

Unfortunately, unsustainable expectations of self-control and perfection don't just go away as we age, especially for women. In fact, you may notice increases in feelings of guilt during the many transitions you experience over time, such as children moving away from home or if you are contemplating retirement. Ultimately, as you age, the only constant in your life will be change. Expecting to travel down this bumpy road with perfect equanimity is likely to lead to painful guilt and disappointment.

From a cellular level to your role in society, you are not the same woman year after year. However, somehow you may have absorbed the expectation that you must live life with zero outward appearance of aging, not to mention any slowing of your thoughts or movements or shifts in desires or interests. It's not hard to absorb this messaging—just look at the proliferation of antiaging skin creams, magazine articles touting exercises to optimize older bodies with the goal of appearing younger, and increasingly public discussions of Botox and a variety of cosmetic surgeries to alter the natural changes accompanying aging. It makes sense that so many of us are scrambling to try to "overcome" this biological process.

You might add expectations about how you should feel when you enter these new phases in your life. For example, if you and your spouse are now home alone, you may suddenly feel pressure to reignite the romance or plan enviable travel or social engagements. You may tell yourself you shouldn't be grieving your children moving on, and that you are wasting your time feeling sad. Or perhaps you expected to feel more relaxed or content in your later years, but you notice heightened anxiety throughout menopause or you become depressed as you try to cope with the illnesses and losses of close friends and family members. Expecting a certain outcome and feeling something different, you may notice the guilt is as high as ever. This is why an awareness of the continued expectation for perfection is important at any age. It doesn't just go away.

The Perfect Career

> "All of my colleagues seem more successful than me. Maybe I'm just not cut out for this role."

When it comes to work and your career, expectations about what you should be enjoying or what you should find interesting can interfere with your true path to authentic engagement. Perhaps you believe you're not working in a job that is important or valuable enough, comparing yourself to some other ideal person and viewing your work as unimportant, as "just a way to pay the bills." This hierarchy of career value creates expectations that are—once again—unfair and unattainable.

Maybe, on the surface, society actually views your work as important but you just don't want to continue along the same path, experiencing intense guilt for having the desire to walk away. For example, you may feel selfish for leaving a job that is seen as caring and meaningful, such as teaching or working at a nonprofit, for something different that is more authentic and exciting for you or that you believe will help you feel less overwhelmed or burned out.

Maybe you gauge your everyday efforts by how closely they match an idealized version of productivity. For example, you may really enjoy your job, finding deep meaning in the relationships you're building, the mentorship you're providing, or the skills you're demonstrating, but you always feel like you should be doing more, working harder, trying to be productive enough.

Additionally, you may carry the belief that your ability to have a successful career comes at the expense of other goals and desires, such as those in your personal life. You may limit the time and energy you place in one area of your life because you don't believe you can have what you want and still be successful. For example, you rarely date, even though you are interested in finding a loving partner, because your work hours would require a flexible option for time together, and you don't think anyone would be willing to comply. Or maybe you would love to start a new business, but you believe your partner would be unhappy if you were away when they came home from work or if you couldn't join them for their own work travel, and this would mean you were a bad girlfriend.

In truth, there are *so* many ways you can find joy in your life, by allowing yourself to spend your time and energy in authentically engaging ways and shedding the expectations of society, your friends and family, even your younger self. Your investment in your career, your family, or other activities does not need to trap you in an endless cycle of burnout and dissatisfaction. Yes, it takes courage to shift energy from what is expected toward what you desire. However, meaningful change is best created by individuals pursuing their authentic lives aligned with their skills and interests, to the very best of their ability. Enthusiasm, curiosity, inspiration: These are not limited to any particular role.

Trying to Have It All: I Can and Should Be Everything to Everyone

Ah yes, the subject of many, many articles about the modern woman: Can she truly have it all?

Yes, women may have more opportunities to pursue meaningful work outside the home, but as we've learned so far, there has not been an equivalent shift to relieve us of the many traditional roles put in place during an earlier era, particularly around housework and childcare. So even if you could have it all—which is a big if—you'd still need to find a way to *do* it all.

Striving for some middle ground, attempting to reach the ever-elusive goal of balance, you may feel perpetually overwhelmed as you carry the burdens of women in early generations while trying to add those previously held exclusively by men. For example, if you try to become the modern Ideal Woman, you are expected to be an impossible combination of traits and talents: caring, cheerful, committed to your family, infinitely patient, sensitive to the needs of others without having too many needs yourself, adept (and enthusiastic) about cooking, highly organized while optimally entertaining, attractive per the current—and continually shifting—ideal, extremely fertile, and willing to prioritize motherhood above all other roles.

But wait, there's more.

You must also be fully in control of your diet, body, mood, appetites, and desires, but never trying to control others; free from any noticeable influence of hormones, menstruation, pregnancy, breastfeeding, or menopause; willing to accept responsibility for the feelings of all your loved ones; able to carry everyone's calendars in your mind; socially active and mentally engaged in meaningful work or volunteering; ambitious but not overly so; and definitely willing to shave your legs every single day, even when it's really cold out and you're just going to wear pants anyway. Is it any wonder you're often exhausted and overwhelmed?

Here is what I want this laundry list of "feminine traits" to illustrate: You can't *possibly* win when you are asked to be superhuman. Perpetually falling short of an unreachable ideal is not the same thing as failing.

Which doesn't mean we don't try. We do try—a lot, usually in the name of work-life balance. However, even this idea— seemingly helpful on the surface—is highly gendered and unfavorable toward women, often assuming that women are balancing employment with childcare duties. There is rarely mention of other activities outside these two areas, and it would make sense for you to ask, "If the *life* part of a work-life balance is all about kids, am I otherwise just left with work?"[8] Limiting the definition of *life* to child-rearing overlooks everything else: relationships with your partner, friends, and family; volunteer activities; great sex; pleasurable hobbies; and healthy habits such as exercise or meditation. Plus, how often are men asked how they balance it all?

Hopefully, as these stereotypes continue to shift, so will the expectations placed on us by the world. We know that when it comes to identity, representation matters. The more women push back on these old-fashioned definitions, choosing instead to create a life of meaning in whatever way appeals to them, the more the rest of us will feel empowered to forge our own path. As you lower your guilt and learn how to move forward with agency, you will become your own trailblazer, seeking authentic goals and living a full and engaged life, however you choose to define it.

So far, we've explored the structural constructs that are asking women to be superhuman, which show up in your life via the socialization you receive from your earliest years and are reinforced by your closest relationships. You have learned about the Four Furies of unrealistic, damaging expectations—Constant Caretaking, Hyper-Accountability, Seeking Perfection, and Trying to Have It All—and recognize you are not alone in your encounters with them. You now see how you've been taught and pressured to become a caretaker for everyone in your orbit, often at your own expense. You recognize the painful, impossible responsibility you've been carrying to identify and fix the emotions of your loved ones. You're aware of the constant pressure to be perfect in your appearance, mood, sexuality, and aging. Finally, you see how the unachievable expectation of having it all is keeping your guilt sky-high.

Unfortunately, guilt and self-criticism have become our way of coping with an uneven playing field. By taking the blame, we create the illusion of control, but as we have discussed, this is an adaptation that is no longer serving us. As you relinquish these constant feelings of guilt, you may feel empowered to push back on the stereotypes still remaining. You can return to our ancient, evolutionarily adaptive skills of collaboration, communication, and support to make some serious progress for future generations of women, as well as in our own lives. You deserve to be seen as you truly are, and you are remarkable.

Why Guilt Is So Sticky—and How We Can Get Unstuck

I n my more than a decade as a clinician, I've seen a similar pattern play out in almost all my patients' lives: Even though they describe something as harmful to them, they find it nearly impossible to let it go. What we must explore in these situations is not just why that habit is causing problems but also how those choices might actually be providing some hidden benefit.

Consider my client Melanie. She told me, "I really want to stop spending so much time on social media after dinner. I just zone out and don't get anything else done."

So I gave her an assignment. "Later tonight, after dinner, sit down in your usual chair but instead of grabbing your phone, just hang out there with your thoughts for a minute."

"Sure, I think I can handle that."

I checked on her progress at our next session.

"Um, it was actually way harder than I expected. I felt really lonely all evening, and I still didn't get much done."

After digging into it, we realized the social media scrolling was serving an important function for Melanie: It was helping her feel connected to other people while distracting her from the painful feelings of loneliness and boredom just under the surface. I asked her if, having recognized this, giving up social media at night was still her goal.

"Yes. It may be helping a little, but I think it's just covering up some loneliness. Maybe instead, I'll try calling a friend in the evening or make plans to meet a colleague after work."

Even though the scrolling was providing Melanie a small benefit by numbing her sadness, it was also interfering with activities and choices that were much more likely to fulfill her needs.

Excessive guilt works the same way. It feels awful and creates painful feelings of self-blame and criticism. It pushes you to strive for impossible perfection and steers you away from your most authentic goals, desires, and connections. It's bad for us in so many ways. So why is it so hard to let it go? Why can't you just tell yourself, "Stop feeling guilty," and *poof,* it goes away? Of course, part of the reason has to do with how challenging it is to lower the outsize expectations your friends, family, colleagues, and society as a whole reinforce every single day. But you can't start chipping away at guilt without acknowledging an uncomfortable yet necessary truth: You might be relying on guilt to help you in a number of ways.

Guilt may be your secret weapon when you are really struggling to get going. You might tell yourself you'd better clean up your messy apartment or your friends will be disgusted by you and think you're a slob. Or that you're a complete failure unless you make it to that early-morning class, and this somehow propels you out of bed. Guilt might also be your way of reassuring yourself that you care, because if you didn't, you wouldn't feel so guilty for missing your friend's birthday dinner (right?).

This is why your brain is constantly telling you that you *need* the guilt to survive. To its credit, your brain is capable of learning new things every day, with the end goal of keeping you safe. When it believes something is protecting or helping you in some way, even via our painful, toxic levels of guilt, it hangs on with an iron grip. So as you consider the many ways guilt presents like a helpful ally in the moment, you must also remember how expensive it can be over the long run. A guilt-ridden life costs you your energy, enthusiasm, self-confidence, and agency—and you certainly aren't getting your money's worth.

Though this list is by no means comprehensive, here are some of the most common benefits guilt may provide—or at least, that's what it wants you to believe.

Guilt Motivates Us

One of the biggest upsides of guilt—and a major reason many of us find it so hard to let go—is that, well, it can be a really effective motivator. In the face of overwhelming expectations, guilt pushes you to do the things you believe you should do. Because guilt feels bad, most of us will do just about anything to remove its grip from our psyche as quickly as possible. Perhaps you believe that if you are in a constant state of self-reproach, you will finally feel motivated to reach the elusive state of being "enough." These judgments, though, are never-ending, because perfection is simply not an achievable goal.

Also, when you use guilt as a motivator, it may work in the short term, but it often leads you to make decisions that are at odds with your true needs and desires. Instead of setting limits on your time so you can finally start updating your CV to apply for a new and exciting role, you agree to work extra shifts at your current job because you feel guilty saying no to your manager. You might feel so guilty about having dinner with a friend and missing the kids' bedtime, you stay up until midnight to prepare everyone's lunch *and* dinner for the following day. Notice how this also can contribute to the over-functioning we discussed earlier?

Another downside to relying on guilt for motivation is that, as you can see, it requires you to feel bad about yourself in order to make the desired change. Remember manipulation, one of the maladaptive forms of guilt? Well, manipulating yourself into behavioral change is most certainly maladaptive, because it forces you to believe you've already done something wrong. Whether it's your approach to taking care of your body or the fact that you haven't finished a project you think you should have finished, motivation via guilt forces you to believe you are starting from behind. You're telling yourself you got it wrong, and now you must make it right. But focusing on your perceived flaws hurts, just as it would if someone important to you was making cruel statements about your choices. You're creating this intense disappointment in yourself, wishing you had acted differently. It can feel demoralizing, like being kicked when you're already down. Do you actually believe this will help you move forward?

What happens is that over time, rather than encouraging goal-directed behavior, guilt may cause you to start rebelling against your own best interests. You may grow really tired of feeling awful all the time and decide it's not the guilt causing all this misery, it's the effort. You just need to stop trying so hard to make positive choices and you won't feel so bad about yourself all the time. You may even turn to unhealthy coping mechanisms to manage the negative experience of guilt, such as avoidance, isolation, or numbing yourself with social media, food, shopping, or alcohol.

What if, instead, you didn't rely on guilt to do the things you want to do? What if you believed you haven't actually gotten anything wrong? What if you planned a particular activity, but then decided to spend your time elsewhere—and you allowed yourself to be OK with it? Maybe an alternative motivational strategy could allow you to start from a place of "I am strong and wise and I want to make this decision" instead of "I mess everything up. I should have known this is what I wanted to do." How differently would you feel if you told yourself, "I haven't done that *yet*, but I'm committed to starting today"? After all, there's a reason Nike's motto is "Just do it" and not "I would have done it already if I weren't so lazy."

Admittedly, this would be a very different book if harsh, punitive thoughts or excessive guilt actually did what you expect them to do: motivate you to grow and make positive changes. However, rest assured, this is most definitely *not* the case. Excessive guilt is ultimately not motivating. It makes you feel smaller, less capable, and less qualified to lead yourself toward positive change, affecting your confidence far into the future. Instead, by finding ways to adjust your expectations, quiet this critical voice, and shift control to agency, you can make the desired transformation in your life.

Guilt Distracts Us from More Difficult Emotions

Elizabeth recently moved back in with her parents. She'd just gone through a difficult breakup while finishing a master's program and needed to start looking for a job. She reached out to me because she had been feeling down and was struggling to find motivation to keep sending out her CV.

Throughout our sessions, the emotion that kept coming up again and again is one you know well: guilt. Not only did Elizabeth feel guilty for living at home and, as she described it, "burdening my parents," she also felt guilty for having other feelings, like frustration, thinking, "I should feel more grateful for what I do have. My parents are being really generous, and I know they're trying their best."

But I suspected that underneath the guilt, there were other, more difficult emotions Elizabeth was trying to keep at bay. So I worked on helping her dig deeper.

"When I sit down to apply for yet another job, I feel so guilty."

"Can you tell me a little more about how you're feeling in those moments?" I asked.

"I don't know. Maybe frustrated and anxious?" she said.

"OK, can you tell me more about that?"

"It's hard, because I know I should be trying to keep a positive attitude, but it's really exhausting and I'm worried I'll never find a job. Then, when my mom asks me to help her with something, I can be kind of a jerk, so I end up feeling guilty."

"That sounds really frustrating."

The more we dug into the guilt, the more we made room for Elizabeth's true emotions—and she was able to notice the unreasonable expectations fueling both. She noticed she held particularly unfair expectations around her interactions with her parents, believing a good daughter would always express gratitude and never seem frustrated or annoyed, even when she was. She also recognized the unreasonable expectations she had about finding the "perfect" job right away, if she could just write the perfect cover letter.

After we identified some of her outsize expectations, I encouraged Elizabeth to take another look at the story she was telling herself about her efforts and accomplishments. Was her perceived reality accurate? She started to realize how unfair she was being to herself. She had overlooked the time and effort she had devoted to getting her master's degree, as well as the ways she had been helping her parents with tasks around the house. As the guilt lessened, she also described feeling really sad, finally allowing herself to grieve her recent, painful breakup.

Growing up, you may have learned, as children often do, that the best way to cope with difficult feelings was to try to make them disappear. You were taught that certain emotions—anger, sadness, anxiety—were dangerous or destructive in some way. Maybe you were told "It doesn't hurt" when a bruise absolutely did, or "You're fine" when you most certainly were not, or "There's nothing to feel anxious about. Just relax" when your distress made relaxing seem next to impossible. So now you invest enormous psychological and physical energy in trying to control or even avoid these negative feelings.

One way our mind tries to avoid or control these unwanted emotions is through guilt. Although this is an uncomfortable emotion, for many of us it is preferable to other feelings, such as sadness or anxiety, as was the case for Elizabeth, and other emotions that are considered bad or inappropriate, especially for women.

Take anger as an example. This is a complicated emotion for women, both when you experience it and certainly if you attempt to express it. You may have learned throughout your life that anger was dangerous, unwarranted, or even unfeminine. The risk of conforming to negative stereotypes about "angry women"—especially for women of color—can pressure you into hiding your anger. Therefore, if you feel emotions you believe are unwanted or disruptive to others, your instinct may be to try to shut them down. Guilt helps you do that. It serves as a noisy distraction. "I shouldn't get so upset when my boss keeps me off interesting assignments because of my limited mobility. She's just trying to protect me. I'm overreacting."

Why would this seem so helpful? Because if you don't express anger, you can continue being the Ideal Woman. You can meet the societal expectations that ask you to prioritize the needs of others above your own and maintain perfect control over your emotions. You can also prevent uncertainty about how the other person would react to your true feelings.

However, what actually ends up happening is that you lose out on addressing the real problem. Instead of telling your supervisor you are perfectly capable of taking on challenging assignments, you hold your tongue, missing out on possible career growth because you don't want to rock the boat. Maybe your mother upsets you when she makes comments about your weight, and instead of asking her not to do that anymore, you stay quiet because you believe you shouldn't be angry. Therefore, she continues putting you down, and you keep feeling bad about yourself, angry—and guilty.

Over time, you may substitute guilt so quickly for another emotion, you don't even realize it. You bury your sadness about your friend moving away in guilt over the fact that you didn't help her pack. You hide your disappointment about losing out on your dream job by creating guilty thoughts about leaving your current role while you're still needed there. You respond to the loneliness you experience as your children leave home by feeling guilty for not planning the perfect family trip. Yes, you are briefly protected from feeling whatever emotion seems most painful or difficult, but it comes at a cost. You can't process or address these important emotional signals unless you are able to clarify your true feelings.

Because the reality is, there are no inherently good or bad emotions. You experience emotions because you exist. Yes, some may seem more difficult to tolerate, but relying on guilt to push them down, ignoring certain feelings, and trying to perfectly control your responses to the world around you always backfires in the end. In this way, guilt blocks your emotional growth.

That's why learning to name your feelings, even when they are painful or undesired, is so important. Adding guilt to an already difficult emotion is like pouring gasoline on a kitchen fire. It just makes everything worse, and even harder to manage.

Guilt Protects Us from the Vulnerability of Feeling Too Happy

Our socialization to be the Ideal Woman can trigger an inner tension whenever you feel "too" happy. To be too happy means to place yourself and your needs before anyone else's—which is not what an Ideal Woman does. In this way, positive emotions can actually feel quite threatening. Therefore, you might start scanning for all the ways you aren't doing well or aren't perfect, and then guilt brings you back down to earth. You say to yourself, "Yes, I got the promotion, but I shouldn't be happy when I know I've been less present in my relationship." This deflating message can also come from people in your life when they notice you are happy. Maybe your parents respond to your news about your pregnancy with concern about your finances, or your spouse chooses to tell you he thinks the house is too messy as soon as you return from an awesome girls' weekend. Don't get used to all this happiness, you're reminded.

Just as guilt can help you avoid addressing uncomfortable emotions, it may also help you offset the discomfort happiness can sometimes bring, by creating feelings of uncertainty about how long it might last or by signaling when you are feeling happy at the wrong time, such as when someone else is unhappy. Unfortunately, because you have been taught to prioritize others before yourself, it can feel like the "wrong time" quite a lot. For example, you might feel selfish for being so excited about a recent first date when your friend just got dumped.

In this way, guilt is a kind of protection, so if your happiness fades, you've prepared for it already. For example, you receive great news about a job interview, but then you remind yourself it would require upsetting your family by moving to a new city, so if you don't get the job, it's probably better in the long run.

What this use of guilt as protection suggests, incorrectly, is that guilt can help you avoid pain, or at least prepare you to cope with disappointment and loss. However, guilt is *not* insurance against difficult emotions. If you fall deeply in love with a romantic partner, feeling guilty for your good fortune will not prevent you from future heartbreak if the relationship ends. Yes, it is vulnerable to deeply enjoy your life and to appreciate the gifts you have been given. Having a life you cherish means you will feel pain if loss occurs. Rather than falling back on guilt to shelter you from this awareness, however, you can move toward acceptance. Life is impermanent, but this can be a source of gratitude rather than fear, and you are stronger than you realize.

Guilt Protects Us from Judgment

You may notice, even as you challenge yourself and seek new opportunities, you also find it necessary to maintain constant vigilance about the risk of appearing too ambitious or successful and thus invoking the judgment of others. Guilt becomes a helpful way to signal that, so that even though it seems like you're doing well, you aren't self-congratulatory or too successful. You aren't a threat, and you're not contributing to others feeling bad. In other words, you're still the Ideal Woman.

So you point out all the ways you aren't meeting certain expectations. You voice guilt about missing your daughter's recital because you were away on a work trip due to a recent promotion. You point out your inability to cook a homemade dinner when someone compliments your presentation at an office meeting. Instead of saying thank you when someone says they admire your work, you deflect and express guilt about your office being messy.

Feeling guilty for your success is *not* true humility. This comes, instead, by acknowledging the variety of resources and privileges you may have had along the way to help you reach success, while also accepting credit for your hard work and achievements. Otherwise, not only are you minimizing your perceptions of your accomplishments—remember the reality part of the Guilt Equation?—but you are perpetuating an unhelpful and unfair model for how a successful woman should act. You are reinforcing the sky-high expectations so many women feel, and harming yourself in the process. This is costly, both for your self-esteem and for the women coming behind you.

Let's begin taking steps toward normalizing pride in our talents and achievements, trusting that those in our orbit can support us through the tough times *as well as* the successful ones, and recognizing we can handle the disappointment if things don't go as well as expected.

Guilt Helps Us Prove We Care Enough

As you learned in chapter 1, showing care is one of the prosocial functions of guilt. If you feel guilty for something you did wrong, seeing your guilt reassures the other person that you value them and their feelings. It can also help you move toward repair and deeper connection. However, as we've seen throughout this book, moderation here is definitely key. When you begin demonstrating your love through *constant* guilt, it ceases to be adaptive.

There's probably no place where this shows up more than in parenthood. It can be overwhelming to adjust to the arrival of a new family member who depends on you for everything. This intense love can bring about powerful emotions, as well as a strong desire to make sure nothing goes wrong. However, you may notice that over time, feeling guilty becomes synonymous with caring. You believe you're a loving mother, so therefore you must blame yourself for anything that goes wrong: "I feel so awful that she caught a cold. I shouldn't have taken her to that play group." Over time, you become hypervigilant about every aspect of your role as a mother and feel perpetually guilty about your inability to do things perfectly—at least, in your eyes. It's understandable, of course, to want to raise a happy and healthy child. However, proving to yourself that you love your child by feeling guilty any time you perceive you aren't doing enough, aren't present enough, or aren't caring enough creates real suffering. What we perceive as enough is not a fixed idea, and it's influenced by so many unrealistic examples of motherhood in the world, particularly online.

Proving to yourself that you love deeply enough by living with constant guilt can also have a negative impact on the recipient of your care. For example, if you express guilt even when you haven't actually created any harm, this can actually make other people feel worse. Let's say you have a friend who is going through a difficult time after being laid off from her job. You recognize she is suffering, and you would like to help her feel better. It would be understandable to feel some guilt regarding your continued stable employment or perhaps your greater financial flexibility. However, repeatedly telling your friend how terrible *you* feel about her circumstances compared with yours is the opposite of helpful. If you say, "I feel so guilty you lost your job while mine is going so well," she may believe she needs to respond to your feeling of guilt, rather than processing her own sadness and frustration. Do you really want to ask her to comfort you when she's already suffering? I imagine this is the opposite of your goal in spending time with her. Instead of guilt, then, you could focus your attention on her experiences, putting your energy into sharing support and compassion, rather than burdening her with your own, unhelpful guilt.

It's not easy to let go of this expectation of constant caretaking. You might believe guilt shows how much you care because the reality is, whenever you actually take time for yourself, you feel like you're being selfish. In addition, because you've been working so hard to take care of everyone else, you might find it difficult to figure out what to do with any available free time. I often hear this from women when they are starting to consider a change. "Honestly, I don't even know what feels fun to me anymore."

However, what if you were to choose the alternative approach of not feeling guilty for having time to yourself? You could focus your energy and attention on rediscovering your sense of play, a path to true relaxation, or a previously treasured activity. You could refuse to punish yourself for having human needs and interests outside your role as a caretaker. You could also model for others in your life the benefits of exploration and self-nurturance, by making choices that leave you reenergized or less stressed rather than sheepishly guilty for the time you took for yourself. You can also support others in the future when they want to take a similar path. This could be the legacy you share—not one of punishment, self-condemnation, and guilt.

Guilt Helps Us Control How Others Respond

When you make choices that don't align with others' expectations of an Ideal Woman—such as doing something for yourself rather than caretaking or setting firm boundaries on extra projects at work—guilt reassures you, as well as those around you, that you know what you "should" be doing. It's almost like you preempt people's disappointment or disapproval with your own guilt, protecting you from their response to your decisions. Maybe you express guilt about missing a family dinner and tell your siblings how terrible you feel for letting them down: "I'm the worst." Then, instead of them responding with, "You let us down," they might actually be induced to reassure you: "Don't worry about it. We can tell that missing our dinner was hard for you."

In this way, guilt serves as a self-imposed punishment to reassure others that you realize you've stepped "out of bounds." Also, importantly, it tells them that because you already feel terrible, there's no need for them to punish you further. This type of performative guilt is a way to "make sure" others will still like you, even when you don't conform to their expectations.

However, let's take a moment to consider likability. This is a tricky one. Do you, like many of us, find the idea of being disliked so distressing that you contort yourself into a shape-shifting people pleaser, no matter the cost, to try to seek others' approval? Maybe you conform to the most likable version of yourself, then apply heaps of guilt to any decision that doesn't align with this goal. That way, at least you are signaling to others, "Don't worry, I'm punishing myself for this breach of the likability contract."

Let me share a personal example of the challenge of focusing primarily on likability. In health care today, the attempt to improve the patient experience has had positive effects, but the proliferation of feedback questionnaires has its downside. In my field, psychiatry, a conflict often occurs. To satisfy a patient, I may be asked to make decisions that I strongly believe will be harmful to them. A medication they want for insomnia will make their sleep worse in the long run, a treatment for anxiety will make it much harder to maintain their sobriety, or continued avoidance to reduce immediate distress will trap them in a life of isolation and suffering.

As a result, throughout my career, I've had many patients disagree with my recommendations. And I'm sure that if asked, they would not rank me as "highly likable." But that's the conflict. If I'm good at what I do—making decisions that align with research into what actually makes people better, rather than agreeing to requests that I know will not serve them—I will not be liked.

But I will be effective.

What if you shifted your goal from being liked to something more powerful, such as being respected or trusted? You would draw people to you who value your opinions, seek your guidance, and believe you make decisions with integrity and compassion. This is what it will look like when you shift from guilt to agency. Are there risks there? Yes, of course. You cannot control the thoughts and actions of the important people in your life, and they might express opinions you really don't want to hear. However, you must work on seeing others as responsible for their own choices, which are outside your control.

The short-term discomfort of vulnerability or conflict may seem unnecessary, even damaging, unless you can imagine the payoff down the road, in the form of increased satisfaction in your authentic decisions and a meaningful deepening of your closest relationships. Remember, your needs and desires are important, and you can set boundaries on your time and energy without burdening yourself with a ton of guilt.

Expecting yourself to always meet everyone else's expectations and prioritizing the happiness or comfort of others above your own quiets your true desires and wishes, letting the needs of others define your path. Remember, you—not guilt—write the script now. You get to decide how you choose to move forward.

⁂

If you've been able to see your own experience in any or all of these functions of guilt, you're not alone. Many of us have spent years relying on self-critical thoughts and sky-high expectations for motivation, control, identity, and self-worth, even though they made us feel terrible. The idea of moving through the world differently can create uncertainty. If we relinquish this performative guilt, will we be seen by others as the worst of the many gendered stereotypes—as an irrational, self-centered, or moody woman? After all, guilt has been our way to demonstrate our understanding of how a woman is supposed to act and feel.

Some of us may also worry about a different consequence of lowering excess guilt: losing control. What if I stop using guilt to jump-start healthy activities and I just end up spending all day in bed? What if I start setting limits on my time, and eventually I've turned down so many invitations, nobody reaches out to me anymore? What if I start asking for what I actually want and I turn into a totally selfish person?

If this is you, here's what I have to say:

Yes, relinquishing the constant stream of self-critical thoughts can leave you feeling vulnerable. This voice has been your companion throughout your life, and you may believe it's the reason you've succeeded and made healthy choices in the past. In its absence, you may have a catastrophic fear of either hiding under a blanket and never emerging or turning into some kind of entitled monster, stomping around demanding everyone's attention and driving your loved ones far, far away.

But remember, excessive guilt is how your brain tries to keep you under control. It tends to focus on worst-case scenarios, and it's very good at getting your attention that way. However, the risk of these extremes is much, much lower than your worried mind tells you it is. Yes, if you never considered anyone before yourself, that wouldn't be good. However, most of us are probably pretty far down on the opposite end, so you can start by simply putting your needs somewhere in the mix, rather than dead last. Catastrophic thoughts about overwhelming losses or rejection from loved ones can be seen for what they really are: anxiety about making a major change toward a life with less guilt.

I encourage you to consider an alternative view when it comes to our dependency on self-criticism and guilt: Throughout your life, you have made choices that are good for your body and mind *despite* this harsh inner critic. You've probably noticed your energy is much higher when you choose to spend time doing something you absolutely love, rather than the activities you just tolerate. You recognize a positive change in your approach to your health when you tell yourself you're working hard to make good choices, rather than criticize yourself for any minor misstep. You may also find your interactions with loved ones go more smoothly when you express your actual needs and encourage them to express their own.

When you lower your intense guilt and stop trying to block your brutal inner monologue with distractions—whether it's social media, food, or overworking—you gain the intellectual and emotional space to build a life focused on what you really want. Guilt is noisy, but moments when you can actually hear your true wishes allow you to make your best decisions.

Your goal for this process of lowering excessive guilt is to expand the time when your unwanted, critical voice shifts into the background, allowing you to make decisions based on how you want to live your life instead of making choices based on what you think you *should* be doing or what you think will guarantee you will be well-liked. You will begin to reap the benefits of this approach as you witness the difference in your own life when you set limits, protect your precious time and energy, and ask for what you need. Important people in your life might push back on these healthy changes, perhaps by echoing your previously critical inner monologue, and it may be tempting to fall in line. However, lowering guilt will give you so much back, whether others ultimately accept it or not.

With that, let's move on to one of the most powerful motivators that exists: self-compassion.

Self-Compassion: A Better Motivator

More than guilt or brutal self-criticism, self-compassion has been proven to be one of the most effective motivators for making positive change. Dr. Kristin Neff, an associate professor in educational psychology at the University of Texas at Austin, defines self-compassion as consisting of three key components:

1. **Practicing self-kindness rather than harsh self-criticism.** Instead of telling yourself, "I can't get anything right," you might say, "That didn't go as I intended, but I know I tried my best and I plan to try again."

2. **Seeing yourself as part of a larger, common humanity, rather than an isolated individual facing the challenges alone.** Rather than saying, "Why can't I even follow a diet like other women? I have no willpower," you say, "I know that so many women experience guilt about the food choices they make, just like I do. It's OK that I feel this way sometimes, even though it's painful. I'm not giving up."

3. **Practicing mindfulness to hold your painful thoughts and feelings in awareness, rather than overidentifying with them.** If you notice a thought like, "I'm not in a relationship because I'm unlovable," which is filled with shame, you instead tell yourself, "I feel lonely today, which is really hard, but I know it won't be this way forever. How can I care for myself right now?"

Maybe the idea that these three simple concepts can be so helpful comes as a surprise to you, because you've always relied on guilt to force yourself into making a "positive" choice. Maybe you worry that if you stop motivating yourself through criticism, you will be less likely to make desired changes. However, the data on self-compassion is clear. In a series of experiments, researchers at the University of California, Berkeley, found that undergraduate subjects completing a brief self-compassion exercise—which involved writing a paragraph to themselves to express kindness and understanding for what they had listed as their greatest weakness or a prior transgression—described more motivation to make positive changes or amends for these events than those who used a positive distraction task, which, in this study, involved describing a hobby they enjoyed in their spare time. Interestingly, the self-compassion exercises were also more likely to motivate change than a self-esteem exercise, in which the students were asked to write to themselves emphasizing their positive attributes and deemphasizing the negative ones.[1]

Think about that. If you're treating yourself with patience and kindness, you are even *better* able to make healthy choices than if you focus on your most positive traits and downplay the negative ones. Remember, your brain is always trying to safeguard you. When you feel like you are under attack—even from your own self-critical thoughts—your brain will find a way to protect you. One of the ways it does this is by shifting to automatic behavior, such as your fight-or-flight mechanism. Instead of thinking clearly, your brain blocks out any information it may find harmful or threatening. When that happens, you are less likely to see yourself clearly, and your perception of reality becomes skewed because you don't feel emotionally safe enough to do so.

However, when you practice self-compassion, you kick-start your ability to see things more accurately. Self-compassion is the reassuring voice telling your brain it doesn't need to hide or plug its ears. You don't need to focus exclusively on your positive traits and ignore the negative ones, like the subjects who were asked to complete the self-esteem exercise in the earlier study. Instead, by staying alert and engaged, you can better understand what might improve things in the future by more accurately viewing what is actually happening right now—in other words, you can recalibrate your Guilt Equation. You can reset your expectations to those that actually serve your best interests. You can see yourself and your reality more clearly and believe you can be "good enough," even if you make mistakes or notice imperfections.

Let's go through an example of how to unlock self-compassion as a powerful motivator. One area with extensive research on the benefits of self-compassion is body image. One interesting study, done by researchers at the University of Denver, involved reviewing the essays of undergraduate women who were asked to write about their bodies with a focus on the three components of self-compassion: self-kindness, seeing yourself as part of something bigger, and mindfulness.[2] Over a period of three weeks, the women followed a weekly twenty-minute writing prompt with quotes such as, "I've got some unhealthy eating habits. I need improving. But I'm not broken." Another said, "You are only given one body in this life so we should love it and treat it with respect." Another participant predicted the benefit of self-compassion: "I think that once you love yourself the way you are it is a lot easier to take control of the situation and change the things that you may not like about yourself."

Compared with women asked to answer a traditional expressive-writing prompt and a control group asked just to reflect on their day, the women who were part of the self-compassion expressive-writing group showed decreases in social comparisons and body shame, as well as decreases in negative social influences, negative health behaviors, and attention to media messages. This is striking when you consider the intervention involved a total of only one hour of self-compassion-focused essay writing.

True body acceptance may seem like a lofty goal, but self-compassion can help you take steps toward it. Returning to the Guilt Equation, you could begin to shift your perception of your body to be more accurate, reminding yourself of the ways your body is working properly, even if it isn't perfect. Rather than viewing your naturally changing body with guilt and self-criticism, you could recognize how you have repeatedly and courageously stepped into the unknown, whether for your first period or the roller coaster of perimenopause, coping along the way with your inherited legacy of renewal. You have survived because you can tolerate a remarkable number of physical and emotional changes, while continuing to care for your loved ones and engage in highly intellectual and athletic feats. Strength and resilience, rather than guilt, are your true legacy. Self-compassion can help remind you of this powerful connection to other women.

Self-compassion can also improve your happiness and health overall. For example, research has noted an inverse relationship between self-compassion and depression and anxiety, meaning the more self-compassion you experience, the less you may struggle with these mental health difficulties. Self-compassion has also been linked to increased levels of happiness, optimism, life satisfaction, and health behaviors.[3] This is a powerful mindset, indeed!

Remember, the way you speak to yourself *matters*, especially when you do something you wish you hadn't. When you catch yourself relying on self-criticism and guilt, try to shift to a more self-compassionate approach. Instead of, "I have no self-control, I'll never make any of the changes I want," practice thinking, "I'm a good person, and I'm trying my best to make positive choices. Tomorrow is another opportunity."

This is not about ignoring the bad and emphasizing only the positive things. It's also not about making excuses for your behavior. Sometimes you will make mistakes, forget to do things you promised you would do, or let someone down, and they will probably be disappointed. This doesn't feel great, and you may decide to apologize or find a way to make it up to them. Self-compassion is about treating yourself with kindness and understanding, *even when you make a mistake*, rather than telling yourself you should be able to do everything perfectly (excessive guilt) or that you are all kinds of awful things (shame). It's about seeing the full picture and still responding with kindness, as well as the belief that you are not alone in this experience.

If practicing self-compassion is difficult for you, as it is for many of us, try this technique: Imagine what you might say to a close friend who's feeling guilty for some act or missed opportunity. This may sound really simple, but I encourage you to try it next time you catch yourself in a negative spiral of self-criticism. It's often much easier to see that a friend—or a child or loved one—who is trying her best is not a terrible person, even when she messes up. By considering the way you would speak to someone you love, you can tap into the part of your brain that feels deep caring and empathy and hasn't been overwhelmed by years of negative self-talk. You might ask yourself how you would encourage a friend who has had a similar setback to your own or one who is struggling to push back against her family's expectations for her choices and behavior. You might imagine encouraging a friend to treat herself with kindness even when she has made a mistake or had to disappoint someone she cared deeply about.

Experimenting with creating distance from your personal experience by imagining a friend also gives you just enough objectivity, a bird's-eye view from outside your head, to respond differently, typically with greater compassion. By resetting your expectations to being *human*—like your friends, rather than perfect like, well, nobody—you can begin to loosen the tight grip of guilt and self-criticism.

In other words, viewing yourself as valuable just as you are is far more helpful and predictive of long-term mental and physical health than the current model of relying on shame and guilt to force change.

❋

Before we move on, let's take a moment to reflect on what you have already learned. You now know a little more about the origins of your excessive guilt and why women seem to be disproportionately affected by it. You've started to recognize how deeply societal expectations of womanhood have been entrenched throughout your earliest years and most important relationships, feeding your experience of guilt. You've considered how the burden of expecting constant self-control has created a need for the self-limiting power of guilt, and you can better understand why lowering your guilt may seem dangerous or leave you feeling vulnerable, especially at first. Finally, you've considered the many ways guilt tricks you into thinking it's helping to protect you, motivate you, and keep you from offending others, when what it's really doing is causing you significant pain.

With this information, you will be able to challenge your self-defeating expectations and tendency to overlook your gifts. You can begin practicing self-compassion and making choices based on agency, truly aligning with your goals and values.

This is a major transformation, requiring self-knowledge and courage, but it's absolutely possible. In fact, in this next section, you will learn about a step-by-step process for lowering all that guilt and replacing it with the empowerment and exhilaration of true agency.

Identifying Your
Guilt Triggers

L et's take a moment to consider a philosophical puzzle. If you are indeed able to adjust your unhelpful or maladaptive thoughts, feelings, and behaviors, as I have witnessed thousands of women do, this creates a challenging question: Who exactly *are* you?

What I mean is, what is the underlying stable force holding firm as you notice and adjust these different aspects of yourself? If you can recognize you are having a guilty thought, who exactly is doing the recognizing?

Your answer is likely influenced by your culture, religion, and other belief structures. You may refer to this true self as your soul, your inner psyche, or the core of your identity. Whatever you choose to call this deep knowing—which exists in all of us, buried underneath layers of unhelpful expectations and habits—it is ready to guide you toward a much more powerful and pleasurable future.

In other words, knowing who you are underneath all this guilt and self-criticism will allow you to finally mobilize true agency.

I'm so inspired by the possibility of agency, rather than guilt, providing a framework for forward momentum. Agency invites you to experience your roles from a place of true empowerment, to be in charge of your own life and feel confident in your path forward. You can use this power to nurture a deep awareness of where you currently stand, revealing the confidence and motivation to intentionally shape your own circumstances. By tapping into this self-knowledge, you can establish a different command center for your life, governed by what you *want* and *need*, rather than what you think you should be doing.

Consider, for a moment, the meticulous care an art conservator applies to the cleaning of a celebrated painting. The challenge of removing layers of accumulated sediment without disrupting the stunning work underneath means they must take their time. The final result is a revelation of the true image, unburdened and undimmed.

I have witnessed women undergo a similar transformation, peeling back the heavy layers of guilt with care and patience, finally emerging as they truly are, and the results are breathtaking.

It is my firm belief that you do *not* have to comply with the world's opinions about how you should live your life. You should also not have to respond to the biases and limitations placed on you in this modern era by striving for unrealistic perfection. You will *never* reach an unimpeachable level of femininity, productivity, or caretaking, no matter how many beauty products or organizational tools you purchase, how many critical remarks you make about yourself, or how many tasks you add to your already endless to-do list. What you can do, instead, is engage with the world differently, beginning with a shift from decision-making based on guilt to authentic choices grounded in agency. If you shift the conversation to problem-solving rather than self-improvement, you can gain confidence and rewrite your own expectations in much more reasonable and helpful ways.

The other important downstream effects of your commitment to lowering guilt by bolstering agency? You will model this change to the women around you. If they can see, reflected in you, their own ability to choose a life that replaces guilt with desire, and likability with respect, they may be more welcoming of this in themselves. Also, crucially, if generational transmission of trauma can occur, it makes sense that generational transmission of *empowerment*, *agency*, and *hope* is also possible. Part of the staying power of guilt involves its widespread use among women, normalizing the presence of this constant emotion. If the message changes, however, and young girls from an early age witness women making decisions based on agency and a balanced approach to their needs and responsibilities, rather than guilt, they will learn how to view the world through a different, more empowering lens.

This means we cannot make decisions based on groupthink. If we do, the status quo—whether it's your willingness to accept responsibility for others' feelings or trying to control yourself with guilt—will always win out.

Until it doesn't.

Eventually, there will be a tipping point, when your continued effort to make authentic decisions in your own life will overtake your years of self-critical thoughts and excessive guilt, opening the door to an incredible transformation. This is the image that helps me approach each day with renewed energy, and it is the perfect place to begin your transformation to a life with less guilt.

SPEAK: How We Build Agency

We begin with SPEAK. After years of helping thousands of women transform their thinking and behaviors away from those pressured by guilt toward those guided by agency and authentic desires, I've boiled down this process of change to five key steps:

Show up

Pay attention

Examine your thoughts, feelings, and behaviors

Take **A**ction

Keep going

I chose the acronym SPEAK for several reasons.

One, I wanted to optimize our memory by grouping key concepts into a simple mnemonic—a helpful strategy employed by overwhelmed students everywhere as they try to memorize important information.

Two, these changes cannot be effective without our willingness to communicate differently, both within ourselves and with the world around us.

Third, and most important, I want to emphasize the power of women's voices when we are united toward a common goal.

The first step to building agency is identifying your guilt

triggers, particularly your sky-high expectations, so you can begin quieting them. This is what the first three steps—showing up, paying attention, and examining your thoughts, feelings, and behaviors—are all about, and what we'll be focusing on in this chapter.

Show Up to the Process

If we want to make changes in our life, we have to begin somewhere. So we begin simply: by showing up to this process. This means you are here, reading about agency and considering something new. You are waking up each day with a plan to investigate the role guilt has been playing in your life, consider your expectations and contributions, and demonstrate the courage it takes to make any significant changes.

As women, we are expected to excel at this first step, at least for others. We have been socialized to show up for everyone, putting their needs first and doing everything we can to care for them. A friend breaks up with a partner and needs a shoulder to lean on? You're there. Your kid forgets she volunteered you to bring cookies for tomorrow's school bake sale? OK, that's not great news, but you'll be there (though maybe with Oreos). Your boss schedules a meeting on a Friday afternoon, just to communicate his concern about office morale? You're sitting in your seat, feigning interest so he believes he's gotten through to you.

Showing up is what you have been trained to do. But showing up for yourself? Now that's a different story. To repeatedly and relentlessly show up for yourself, you must push back against years of messaging telling you that to be the Ideal Woman, you need to put others first, to set aside your own needs until later, if at all, and to strive for likability at all costs. However, I'm here to convince you that lowering your guilt does not mean sacrificing your motivation, letting everyone down, or leading an isolated existence. Not only will you feel so much better with less guilt, you will also be a more connected, energized, and confident person. In fact, it will be absolutely life-changing. You may no longer be the Ideal Woman, but you'll be something better—a whole self.

Showing up also means you are willing to pause in your hectic day to consider the variety of ways you are making an effort, facing challenges, and getting things done, which will help you to bolster the reality portion of the Guilt Equation. Because the reality is that you showed up today! Can you recognize the effort it took for you to make time and space for this book? This is no small feat.

By showing up, you are communicating a sense of hope about the potential for change, and you might even start to believe things don't have to be so difficult. Or maybe you're skeptical but willing to give it a try. I think that's terrific. A healthy skepticism toward claims of a life-changing process is not only valid but also extremely wise. A simple willingness to notice your own thoughts and feelings is a courageous start. You are telling yourself your life matters and you are worthy of the time and attention this transformation will require.

Pay Attention to When Guilt Creeps Up

Here are some comments I've heard in my practice:

"My best friend is always doing things for others. She should take some time to rest and reset. I'm sure she's exhausted."

"My partner is so overwhelmed, but he doesn't seem to recognize it. He doesn't have any appetite and his sleep is so restless. He really needs to try to lower his stress."

"My daughter can get so focused on her homework, she doesn't let herself have fun with her friends. I don't think that's healthy, do you?"

"And what about you?" I'll ask.

"No, I'm fine. Whenever I do something for myself, it just seems indulgent, and I feel guilty for not getting other things done."

This is where we begin, by paying attention to when and where guilt shows up and influences our behavior. This next step is really important. If you want to start moving toward a goal, you first have to recognize your current position. Firing up the GPS in your car works because, unless told otherwise, it sets the starting point wherever you are parked.

It's the same with guilt. The path to greater agency begins with getting clear on your starting point: what's triggering your guilt in the first place. If you don't know the unfair expectations that are driving your decision-making, how can you possibly change them? Once you see where you've been placing your valuable attention—such as on your sky-high expectations or the ways you believe you've fallen short—you can start to shift. You can begin directing your attention to more empowering and compassionate thoughts and experiences. Your new focal points become powerful tools to rewrite your relationship with excessive guilt.

Initially, however, you may not even be aware you're experiencing guilt, because your brain so quickly jumps to ways to fix the problem. For example, you immediately offer to chaperone your child's school trip as soon as you receive their teacher's email request, later wondering why you agreed to something you would have definitely preferred to avoid. Taking a moment to look back at the email, you realize what motivated you was guilt. You hit respond as soon as you read, "We know most parents are very busy and can't always volunteer, but the kids are so excited for this trip. I hope we don't have to cancel because we don't have enough supervisors." Yes, under these circumstances, guilt is not an unreasonable emotion, and may even have been the intended effect of that messaging. However, when you take a beat and look inward, you can spot the unhelpful expectation underneath: "I have to help out more at school or else I'm a terrible mother."

So how can we start identifying our guilt triggers? When I'm working with an individual grappling with excessive guilt, I encourage them to scan their thoughts for some key phrases. Words like *never*, *always*, and *should* tend to catch my attention, because they often indicate unrealistic expectations. You might tell yourself, "I can never stick to a healthy diet." Or perhaps, "I always say the wrong thing," or "I should be able to get everything done without feeling so exhausted all the time."

In addition to these key words, watch out for broad generalizations based on one particular circumstance. For example, if you think to yourself, "I'm such a disaster. I can't do anything right," when your only misstep was forgetting the dressing for the salad you brought to a friend's dinner party, this can be a clear indication of unreasonable expectations and dismissed effort. Or perhaps you tell your spouse, "I totally bombed my meeting today. Everyone must think I'm an idiot," when further discussion reveals that although you had been feeling anxious while you were speaking in front of your team, the meeting actually went quite well. This kind of catastrophic thinking can understandably increase toxic guilt, because you are imagining all the dramatic ways you may have failed, rather than noticing what you've accomplished.

If you're experiencing a general feeling of guilt but don't quite know why, follow the progression of your thoughts and behaviors back to the source. Take Nancy. She was getting ready for work, completing the usual tasks to start the day: taking a shower, eating breakfast, and brushing her teeth. However, something seemed different that morning. She noticed she was feeling guilty. How did she know? First, she recognized common guilty thoughts, such as, "You are the worst. Why can't you take care of things like you're supposed to?" This guilt also showed up in her body, causing a tight feeling in her stomach and a dull headache.

Nancy mentally reviewed the past several days but couldn't identify anything to explain this feeling of guilt. It really seemed to have come out of nowhere. Just before she left her apartment, however, she walked past her bed and saw a pile of papers on her nightstand, including a reminder card from the dentist. She remembered looking at this card when her alarm went off that morning but had forgotten about it as she moved on with her day. Now, though, because Nancy's guilt was focusing her attention on what she may have gotten wrong, she noticed the return of this thought: "I can't believe I haven't been to the dentist for three years. I probably have ten cavities."

The guilty feeling increased, and she had her answer. It was the dental card on the nightstand. If she were playing Clue, the mystery would be solved.

Another way to spot your triggers is to notice when you are trying to take responsibility for areas outside your control. "I'm sorry I planned this outdoor event on a day that it rained. I really let everyone down." Can you truly control the weather? Or "I caught this terrible cold right before we were supposed to go away for the weekend. I'm the worst." When did you find a way to prevent the common cold? Or "I ran out and bought my friend the expensive bag she wanted because I had to cancel our plans and she seemed really bummed." Remember what we've learned about why it's counterproductive to try to fix someone's emotional experience or protect them from disappointment? Yet if you often find yourself doing just that, consider whether guilt—at not being a good event planner or a good friend, in these examples—might be driving your decision-making.

It's important to point out that triggers for guilt are far from universal, and not all people will feel the same way in the same settings. It takes time and directed attention to understand why you have your particular triggers. When you're really listening to yourself and experiencing your emotions, you can better recognize the people and activities that trigger excessive guilt or feelings of inadequacy, as well as the ones who can provide measured, helpful suggestions to guide you in your decisions.

When examining your triggers, it's also important to approach them with curiosity and self-compassion, rather than judgment. Let's say you notice guilty thoughts, feelings, or behaviors mostly at night, after you've run out of tasks to try to distract yourself from feeling less than enough. Don't judge, just take notice. Instead of saying, "Why can't I control these guilty thoughts?" consider, "I notice I'm feeling guilty at this moment, and that's OK, but where might this be coming from?" This shift in your thinking will help you explore your thoughts more fully because you won't be having to fend off your brutally critical voice first. Sometimes, just speaking these thoughts out loud or writing them down and reading them back to yourself can help you see them more objectively. It is not uncommon in my sessions to hear someone say, "Wow, now that I'm paying more attention and saying this out loud, I hear how unfair it is. Why would I always need to feel guilty to prove I cared about someone?"

Through repetition, you will eventually notice the curious and compassionate thoughts will start to show up first, rather than the harsh, guilty ones. Why? Your brain is amazingly plastic, meaning it is capable of growing and changing throughout your life, based on your repeated thoughts and actions.

The Neuroscience of Change

Let's take a moment to talk a little bit more about how the brain learns, because this will demonstrate how important it is to direct your attention to self-compassion instead of guilt. When you start paying attention to your guilt triggers, you might ask yourself, "Why is it so difficult to shift my focus toward something more encouraging and less guilt-producing?" Yes, it can be challenging to make this kind of change. This is because your brain is wired with a negativity bias, meaning you are more likely to notice things that didn't go well or flaws in your performance or yourself.[1] In our ancestors, this focus on problems and missteps allowed them to make the adjustments necessary for their continued survival. However, because we live in a very different time and place, we no longer need the same type of vigilance toward everything that has gone or could go wrong. In fact, it is vital to take time to pay attention to the areas where things are on the right track.

The reason why is because the way the brain takes in new information and adds it to our understanding is by first paying attention, using all our senses to gather information. This information creates electrical and chemical reactions in the brain that strengthen connections between the neurons, the brain's primary communication cells. The information is then encoded into memory. The more these neurons are encouraged to communicate with one another, the stronger the bond becomes over time.[2] So if you spend hours categorizing your faults and perceived failures, eventually, that is all you will be able to see.

In fact, creating lasting memories or learning something new is nearly impossible without sustained attention. Why? Because without it, the information never even makes it into the brain in the first place. This means the highly sophisticated steps your brain takes to review the data and store it as learned material and memories can't even begin; there's nothing there to review! But if you pay attention to something repeatedly, your brain lays down a strong and speedy track for this information to reach its destination. You may have experienced this when the lyrics from a song you haven't heard for over a decade pop into your brain. Listening to that song over and over created an enduring memory, with lasting power far beyond something you may have hoped to remember from your classes at school.

What this boils down to is that what you pay attention to over and over again matters. If you repeatedly think, "I should never miss a holiday with my family because that would mean I'm an ungrateful person," it will be more thoroughly learned, and more likely believed. However, if you begin to shift to something more fair, like, "I love my family, even though I can't be at every function. That doesn't mean I'm a bad daughter," over time, you will find other, more compassionate thoughts may come a little more easily, too.

In addition, repetitive attention to thoughts and emotions in a particular context can also lead to a strengthening of neural connections. In fact, the more emotionally salient a thought or feeling is, the more likely key areas of your brain will light up and say, "Hey! We need to remember this!" In this way, an association is formed, also called conditioning.

For example, let's say you've been struggling with insomnia. The worse you sleep, the longer you might try to stay in bed. The unintended effect of this change, however, is that it actually reinforces the unhelpful connection between the bed and upsetting sleeplessness. Eventually you become so conditioned to dread the bedroom, you might feel extremely sleepy on the couch watching TV, only to get into bed and feel wide awake and anxious. Why is this happening? Because the brain remembers! It's saying, "OK, the bedroom is where I come to be awake and anxious. I've got this!" Therefore, part of treating your insomnia involves being in bed only when you feel sleepy, and limiting any anxious time in bed.

Guilt works in the same way. Let's say you decide to start going to the gym three days a week. For the first month, you follow this plan and feel proud of your consistency. "I'm taking such good care of myself!" Each visit to the gym reinforces this positive behavior, because you feel great when you leave, increasing the chance that you will return. However, what if one week you catch a bad cold and you don't go to the gym? When you return after the congestion improves, rather than feeling proud, you feel guilty. "I should have fit in a workout even when I wasn't feeling great. I'm so lazy." You end up leaving the gym feeling disappointed in yourself and guilty for the missed workouts. Your attentive brain notices this new feeling and snaps to attention. "Right! Going to the gym makes me feel bad. Let's stop doing that so I don't feel so awful!"

Same gym, same workout, but a very different thought process. The time and attention you give to your guilt about missed sessions, rather than motivating you, means you now connect the gym with something negative. Your thoughts are *that* powerful. When you repeatedly link certain activities, such as missing a workout, to laziness—or anything else you've been conditioned to believe that women shouldn't be—the negative experience of guilt can stop you from doing it altogether.

Another way to shift your attention away from guilt-fueled thoughts is to ask yourself: What part of today do I believe I did well? Keep a small notebook or an app on your phone handy where you can jot down the things you accomplished that day—remember, they don't always have to be epic. "I finally recycled that pile of newspapers" or "I took the stairs at the office" would both be excellent things to document. In other words, how did you show up for yourself today? Let this list be as visible as your lengthy to-do list, with extra points granted for showing it to someone else.

By paying attention to your guilt triggers and approaching yourself with less criticism and judgment, you begin to rewire yearslong thought patterns in the brain. As you can see, your brain is eager to learn new things. Instead of feeding it a steady diet of self-criticism and evidence of failure through your disproportionate attention to these types of thoughts, shifting to curiosity and a nonjudgmental stance toward yourself can be a powerful change. Not only does your attention matter, but the frequency and intensity of the attention you grant to certain thoughts, feelings, and experiences also affect how you perceive them and even how often they occur.

Examine the Evidence:
What Expectations Are Driving Your Guilt?

Once you've started noticing when, where, and how guilt tends to rear its ugly head, you can move on to examining these triggers to help you understand their origins, perpetuating factors, and the effects these thoughts, feelings, and behaviors have on your daily life.

To begin, ask yourself the following questions:

Is there a clear pattern for the times I notice the most guilt? Does it show up when I'm looking at my full email inbox or after I've finally gotten the kids to bed? Does it pop up after every call with a certain family member?

What kind of environments seem to trigger the most guilt? Home? The office? Out in the world? At my child's school?

In which of my roles do I seem most likely to notice guilt? As a romantic partner? A friend? A parent? An employee?

Do I tend to notice the guilt right away or does it take a little time to figure it out? (This delay can be common, especially at first, but it will decrease with time and practice.)

Why are you asking yourself these questions? Because moving along in the SPEAK process requires a clear assessment of your unique patterns of guilt. Just as you need accurate measurements before you can choose the right clothes, examining the evidence about your particular guilt triggers and how you respond to them is necessary to make better choices in the future. It certainly doesn't help you if the actions you take reflect someone else's experiences with guilt, just as you wouldn't ask for your friend's measurements before ordering yourself a new outfit.

Here's an example of what this examination might look like.

Let's say you've been noticing guilt in the evenings, any time your partner has had a difficult day at work. When he starts sharing some of his challenges, you notice thoughts like, "I should be able to cheer him up. Why can't I think of the right thing to say?" You notice you then respond to this guilt by trying to take care of him, such as by giving him advice about work, cooking dinner, or cleaning up his side of the bedroom. When none of these efforts seem to help, it leads to even more guilt.

After you've examined your thoughts and feelings in this way, you can start digging into the assumptions buried beneath the guilt. You feel guilty, yes, and you realize you also feel like you've failed. Ask yourself, "What, exactly, have I failed at?" Maybe you believe you've failed at being a "good girlfriend." Dig deeper: What does being a good girlfriend mean? Your unreasonable expectations tell you this must mean taking care of your partner's every need and making sure they're always happy. Ask yourself, "Is this a realistic expectation?" No.

Here's another example. Maybe you realize guilt emerges most powerfully whenever you speak to your parents on the phone, especially if they mention they are worried about a health issue or feeling sad about the illness of a close friend. You would hang up and feel awful, telling yourself, "I'm a bad daughter. I'm not doing enough for them." This is such a broad generalization, typically a red flag signaling you've set unfair expectations for yourself and are minimizing your efforts. So again, ask yourself: What are those expectations? A good daughter would always be able to protect her parents from sadness or fear? A good daughter would never feel like she let them down? Are these expectations realistic? No. Of course the resulting guilt is going to be sky-high.

As you begin to examine the roots of your guilt, you might come to realize your triggers fall under one of three buckets: reflected appraisals, comparison, and authentic desire.

Reflected Appraisals

In chapter 2, we learned about reflected appraisals, the lingering effects of how we were viewed and treated as children, which can shape our self-image at an early age and long into adulthood. Understanding the appraisals you're still holding on to can give you powerful insight into what your unique guilt triggers might be.

Begin by asking yourself these questions:

> Were there any particular labels my family gave me as a child or teenager? For example, maybe you were viewed as the superneat, organized one, but this was actually because you felt anxious unless items were tidy, and you also used cleaning to procrastinate. Or maybe you were the athlete, expected to play every sport and maintain a tough exterior.

Looking back, was there a role I played in my family? Or maybe several roles? For example, maybe you cared for your siblings because you were seen as very responsible, or perhaps you rebelled against your parents' restrictive rules on behalf of your quieter siblings. Perhaps you were always telling jokes, trying to keep everyone laughing so your parents wouldn't argue so much.

Would anyone in my life now agree with the labels or roles I was given then? If you asked your spouse or close friend, would they agree that you fit the label you carried as a child? Maybe they see why your parents described you as "always in control," or "a little bit of a space cadet." Or maybe it's just the opposite. Would they be surprised by your label of "slacker" because you're so incredibly driven and productive now?

What do I think about the labels and roles I was given as a child? Can you make any connections between your younger self and the expectations you are setting for yourself now? Maybe you're trying to keep up with a positive label and feeling overwhelmed by the effort. Or perhaps you're constantly scanning your life to make sure you aren't adhering to these negative scripts.

Examining your reflected appraisals is like reading the fine print on your own instruction manual. Perhaps you've shed some of them as you've grown into an adult, but you may also just be unaware of their continued existence. They can become such an automatic framework for your choices, you may not even realize they're present. You immediately take the lead in a family emergency, hiding your own fear or grief, because you are the one who's expected to never show your stress. You hide a recent layoff because you are supposed to be the successful one and you're too embarrassed to ask for much-needed help, even though you know it's available. Guilt creeps up when you fail to meet the expectations set in childhood.

Like lyrics to an old song, these reflected appraisals have a way of getting stuck in our heads, and they may seem impossible to shift. However, they are not written in ink. You have the power to change your response to these tired ideas, whether they pop into your head or they're voiced by someone else. Just knowing they exist allows you to reflect on their accuracy. "I've always been told I'm the screw up, but is that actually true?" Consider evidence that refutes this belief, "Would a screw up have a job she loved?" and remind yourself of the ways you are so much more than your narrow, assigned role. It's absolutely time for you to be the final word in your own unique story.

Comparison

Comparisons can significantly influence the expectations that fuel our guilt because we assume any failure to measure up to others is due to our lack of effort, skill, or commitment—in other words, *If she's able to do it this way, then I have no excuse.* Like most of us, I assume you do this, All. The. Time. It's easy to find examples of people doing amazingly well in a role you sometimes struggle in. You can effortlessly picture that mom in your friend group who is only one week postpartum and looks incredible, while you've only just found the time and energy to take a shower; or a woman at your gym who is an entrepreneur with her own thriving business, while you've only gotten as far as a glitchy website and some business cards.

The worst part is, research suggests we tend to seek out comparisons most often during times of transition or stress—which is also when we are most vulnerable to feeling inferior or believing we have fallen behind.[3] So, you are already frazzled, buried under a never-ending to-do list, with far too few hours in the day to complete it. Then, to make yourself feel really terrible, you decide to compare yourself to someone else. Do you choose a woman who is even more overwhelmed than you are? Do you find someone who has just spent ten hours bingeing a reality series on Netflix? Of course not! You rack your stressed brain to come up with someone you believe has everything figured out, someone who's obviously superior to you in her organization, efficiency, maybe even fashion sense, which makes you feel even worse! Why do so many of us torture ourselves this way?

Similar to guilt, comparison can seem like the ideal motivator. You look for someone who is doing well, start making similar choices in your own life, and soon you will be better, right? Unfortunately, this is the problem with comparisons. You are comparing your internal experiences—including anxiety, uncertainty, and, yes, guilt—to their external version, which may be hiding any number of their own challenges. The new mom you envy is actually focusing on her appearance because she feels totally inept with her new baby. The businesswoman you admire is struggling to grow her company to support herself through a difficult divorce.

Limited resources create competition in most species, and humans are no different. At a biological level, you are designed to compete for the best ways to pass along your unique genes. In modern times, your access to the declared successes and ingenuity of your "peers" is at an all-time high, and the unhelpful comparisons can really pile up, creating intense guilt and self-doubt.

This is important: I have placed *peers* in quotation marks because, like many women, you often believe, usually in error, that your object of comparison has all your strengths in addition to the talents they're highlighting in your interaction or even just on your tiny screen. You also significantly downplay their faults or challenges. In other words, when you choose your object for comparison, you are viewing an optical illusion of a perfect woman, and you can't help falling for it, raising your expectations sky-high. Then, when you believe you are falling short of these idealized examples of productivity, exercise routines, or appearance, your perceived reality tells you that you are failing. So you turn inward, asking yourself to "improve" in exhausting and unrealistic ways, concerned that any missed opportunities are due to poor concentration, limited willpower, or low motivation.

Social media especially can create particularly harmful illusions of perfection in others, fueling comparison tenfold and resulting in negative outcomes. For example, in one interesting study from the Graduate School of Health at the University of Technology Sydney, in Australia, researchers collected the online surveys of 201 mothers to assess the influence of social media on the relationship between their perfectionism and their mental health. The researchers also wanted to know if social support might buffer negative influences of social comparison on these social media sites. The results described a clear link between social comparison and perfectionism and depressive, anxious, and stress symptoms—not too surprising. They also noted that social support seemed to buffer the risks of these comparisons to other mothers on social media, though not entirely. This data tells us that even when we are surrounded by a loving network, these comparisons can still act as powerful triggers for guilt by prompting sky-high expectations, not to mention painful symptoms of depression and anxiety.

So how do we begin to let go of comparison's grip on our expectations? Ask yourself, "Who have I been selecting for comparison, and how accurate are my assumptions? Is she really doing everything perfectly?" Remember, even in those women you see online but don't know personally, complexity is the norm, rather than the exception. It may sound cliché to say nobody is perfect, but this is absolutely true. Maintain a healthy skepticism toward images of perfection, effortless success, and constant happiness because—trust me on this—behind the scenes there are imperfections, hard work, and periods of sadness, pain, and disappointment. How do I know this? Because I've spoken with thousands of women in my psychiatry practice, not to mention those who share their personal stories with me outside the office, and I have never met someone who had it all together in every aspect of her life. Ask any therapist and she or he will say the same thing. This is the true human condition, which no one can fully transcend.

You can do this more naturally in your close relationships. If you find you're comparing yourself to a friend, spend quality time with her. You may start noticing her apparent confidence masks some areas of self-doubt and disappointment. You can begin to know her as a full person. You may still experience envy about an aspect of her life, but you no longer wipe away her full, complex experience to see her only in an idealized social media form. You recognize her as human, with human imperfections.

It takes work to modulate your immediate reaction to images of perfection and success, particularly when you are feeling down or self-conscious about your own choices. Remember, self-comparisons increase during times of stress or insecurity. However, when you start to challenge your assumptions about others, you begin to spot the holes in your airtight theory about what "everyone else is doing." You also begin to learn that the story you tell yourself about everybody else is just your perception.

With that in mind, consider a simple substitution. Instead of "She's perfect," try saying to yourself "She's projecting an image of perfection." Rather than "She's so successful," try "She's projecting an image of success." This is truly *all* you can tell from an online post, reel, or YouTube video, with everything else filled in by your active imagination. However, pointing out what is being projected can help you reset your impression from "She's got it all" to something far more reasonable.

Also, consider this important point: You choose your object for comparison. If you are having a difficult day at work, you might be more likely to pay attention to comparisons that suggest you are unproductive—or in scientific terms, data that supports your hypothesis that you are lazy. Maybe you imagine the workaholic colleague who never seems to go home: "Why do I need to take breaks for meals and sleep? Look at Cheryl, staying here until midnight every night. She's like a machine!" Try the trick you learned earlier: "Cheryl is really projecting an image of a hardworking employee. I'm sure there are challenges she's facing that I don't know about."

By understanding that your perceptions and choices for comparison reflect your underlying mood and self-image, you can start to catch yourself creating unattainable and unrealistic role models. Then, you can consider alternative models for comparisons. Maybe, instead of the Olympic runner, you could compare your fitness level to a regular woman sweating alongside you in your exercise class. Rather than judging the success of your business by how it measures up to the CEO on the cover of a magazine, you instead connect with another small business owner in your community and compare notes on the ups and downs of entrepreneurship.

If you find it difficult to shift from believing the image on-screen to saying "She's really projecting an image of something I want," then it might make sense to practice limiting your exposure to influences with the most toxic effects. This may sound overly simplistic, but it's striking how many times I say this in session, and women reflect on how empowering it would feel.

"I guess I could stop following those Instagram accounts of the women that make me feel like a total failure?"

Um, yes. Please, please do. This is a powerful form of self-care.

Instead, create a feed that makes you smile. Though, admittedly, I have had my own difficulties limiting my social media consumption, I now follow several art museums online, and scrolling down to find a breathtaking piece of art regularly lifts my spirits. Otherwise, I exclusively focus on cute videos of troublemaking puppies and costumed hedgehogs, which I highly recommend.

Additionally, rather than continuing to make these extremely unhelpful comparisons to women online, actually reach out to your true social network, those people who will tell you that you are fabulous and doing a great job, right on track. Why is this important? Because, unlike people responding to the images you put online, your support network knows you far better, your gifts as well as your struggles. It's harder to dismiss positive reinforcement from someone who knows how hard you've been working than it is to disregard a brief "Great job!" post on a social media site. Joining your sister for lunch and laughing about the ridiculous thing that happened when you tried a new exercise class can be a much more effective balm for embarrassment than hearing a stranger's story online. Racking up several "likes" on a post you've written may not feel as good as an encouraging text from a close friend who knows how long it's taken you to achieve your goal.

Some other ideas:

> Text a group of friends a silly meme representing your current frustration, and see if any of them relate.

> Ask a friend to take a walk, and each of you can share the ups and downs of your week.

> Write a letter or email to a friend who lives far away, telling them about something you felt proud of recently. Ask them to respond with a similar story.

> Compliment another woman. Maybe you like her glasses or you enjoyed her talk at the conference or you appreciated how kind she was when she was ringing up your groceries. Then see if you can find a similar compliment to give yourself.

> Compare yourself—favorably—to your younger self in some way. Maybe you are more organized, well-read, confident, or grounded now than you were at one point in the past. How have you improved?

You cannot lower your guilt by comparing yourself to some unattainable ideal. Short of fully unplugging from other people as well as your social media accounts, you can learn to buffer yourself from the onslaught of lives you "should" be living. Keep a close eye on your own responses to online and in-person interactions, and curate an environment that not only supports you but also challenges you to learn and grow toward a life with true depth and meaning, not just the appearance of success.

Authentic Desire

Sometimes, when we imagine a life with less guilt, when we start to acknowledge and live according to our true needs and desires, this ends up triggering still more guilt. We might notice we are setting new boundaries on our time and effort, and worry this isn't what an Ideal Woman would do. For example, maybe you imagine telling your partner you no longer want to stay in the same job and immediately feel guilty for even desiring this change. "They would be so stressed if we didn't have my income while I transitioned into a new career." Perhaps you picture talking to your mother about a new limit on your ability to see her every day and think, "I should just leave things as they are. I'd be selfish to protect my personal time."

Another potent trigger of guilt is when we actually achieve the authentic goals we've set or experience a much desired life transition. You may notice even these kinds of positive changes can evoke feelings of guilt.

For example: You're a new mom, a transition involving not only more responsibility but also much less sleep and time to yourself. Suddenly, this vulnerable infant is counting on you for food and diaper changes, oblivious to your exhaustion, and disinterested in a discussion of the things you miss about your former life. This new family member is so incredibly loved, but that doesn't mean you don't have challenges with the transition. Assuming a totally smooth process and blaming yourself for any difficult feelings just leads to more guilt.

Noticing you are experiencing simultaneous excitement and regret is not uncommon with major changes, but you may believe you shouldn't be feeling a certain way or else it means you are a "bad" version of that role, especially if you have hoped for this change for a long time. If you have very rigid expectations about how a new mother should feel—such as an expectation of constant bliss—this ambivalence can create intense guilt.

Promotions at work are another example of stressful though generally desired events in which you might catch yourself feeling guilty. Through your hard work and demonstration of excellence, you have been rewarded, but sometimes unexpected burdens can occur. Maybe you feel guilty for being promoted ahead of your work friends or when you are taking on new or additional responsibilities, you miss the camaraderie of working closely with the people you are now asked to supervise. Perhaps you have far less time to participate in the hobbies you love, because work is taking up a much larger portion of your waking hours. The guilt may emerge again, because you believe you should only feel happy about the change, which you've worked so hard to achieve.

You may also feel guilty when you feel better than you think you should in a certain situation. For example, as you move forward with much less guilt, you might notice a sense of something missing. The heavy burden of guilt, when it is removed, can leave you feeling a little unsteady, adapting to such a major, though certainly desired, change.

When you notice excessive guilt after a major transition, it can be helpful to take an honest look at the time before the change and give some attention to what you might be missing. Even when it's a desired change, that doesn't mean everything was worse before the transition. It is important to understand what it's been like to give up that old role, including both the positive and the negative changes you've encountered. Importantly, you must try to consider these questions with curiosity, rather than judgment.

Also, keep in mind, expectations about how you should be responding to changes in your life can interfere with the awareness of how you are actually responding. Yes, it may feel vulnerable to admit to feelings of regret or grief, for example, but pretending they don't exist just means they show up in other ways, interfering with your authentic experiences.

This is the challenge and the incredible opportunity of developing agency. You have to admit to yourself that change is necessary in order to live your most satisfying, engaging life. This takes courage because, as with anything new, you have to adjust to the change. Allowing yourself to be human, with a broad range of human emotions, rather than an unattainable Ideal Woman who only feels joy and positivity, is such an important and powerful shift. Most women benefit from validation of the natural ambivalence we may experience during transitions and then examining our self-talk, recognizing where it might be contributing to unhelpful feelings of guilt.

When the guilt begins to lessen, you can better appreciate the rich collection of emotions triggered by major changes in your life and accept both the enjoyable and more challenging aspects of any new experience. You will also likely start showing up differently in your relationships, with the agency to ask for what you want, seek out what you need, and love with your full, empowered self. Yes, it's true that you cannot control the thoughts or feelings of other people in your life, no matter how many times you are told you "should." They are allowed to have their own reactions to your attempts at change, but they don't dictate what is most meaningful or desirable to you. Learning how to navigate this feedback from your social network will be the topic of a future chapter.

Next, after learning about the importance of showing up, paying attention, and examining your thoughts and feelings to better understand yourself and your guilt, you can move on to the next chapter, where you will learn to *take action*. Let's go!

6.

Quieting Your Guilty Thoughts

Now that we've started to identify what triggers our guilt, how do we begin to lower it? It's tempting to try to do so by working even harder. You might tell yourself you will get rid of the guilt by exercising frequently, never letting the laundry pile up, paying those bills early, and calling your parents every day—in other words, by doing the very things your brain tells you that you *should* be doing. But this only amplifies your guilt. How? By taking on more and more responsibility, you elevate your already high expectations even further, while also creating more opportunities to feel like you've failed if you don't succeed perfectly.

Loosening guilt's grip, therefore, must start within, with your ability to quiet your guilty thoughts. Trying to skip these internal changes with frantic activity—literally running away from the guilt—may work for a moment, but like a hungry kid when you're on an important call, the guilty thoughts will just keep showing up to interrupt you. There is no amount of effort that can suppress the guilt forever. What you need, instead, is lasting change—and that starts from within.

In this chapter and the next, we will focus on the fourth step of SPEAK: taking action. We will begin by learning three key concepts that will help us shift our critical, guilt-fueled thoughts: thought restructuring, nurturing a growth mindset, and positive psychology. Applying these strategies can help you adjust both variables of the Guilt Equation—your expectations and your perception of reality—and make powerful internal changes to shift your unhelpful relationship with guilt.

Once we've addressed how we can lower the guilt manifesting in our thoughts, we will explore how to live with less guilt in our relationships. This will involve learning how to set—and keep—reasonable boundaries, how to delegate instead of taking care of everything, and how to live with feelings of disappointment, both in yourself and in others. This will be the topic of the next chapter.

Thought Restructuring

Yes, your thoughts are powerful, and they influence you in many ways. However, *you are more than just your thoughts*. You have the ability to change or rewrite them to create a more realistic and motivating way of thinking.

If your current guilt-ridden thoughts are rough drafts, over-influenced by society's expectations, the reflected appraisals formed by your earliest relationships, your life experiences, and the slow, tempting creep of hyper-competence, consider the new, less guilty thoughts as the edited versions. These will be written to guide you through a life less burdened by sky-high, unrealistic expectations. They will also help you keep your reality accurately updated with the many things you are already doing well.

As we begin restructuring our thoughts, some of the strategies we will use come from a particularly helpful type of psychotherapy many of you may already be familiar with: cognitive behavioral therapy (CBT).[1] CBT was originally developed as a way to help individuals with depression address their negative, self-defeating thoughts. It is now a very popular therapeutic modality used to help with a broad variety of problems, such as obsessive-compulsive disorder, binge-eating disorder, and anxiety disorders, to name just a few. In my work with women, I've used these techniques to help reduce many guilt-ridden thought patterns.

You start by bringing attention to your thoughts, including those that are initially automatic and outside your awareness, such as a fixed expectation of perfection or the immediate assumption that you have done something wrong. Then you begin to notice the thought errors—also referred to as *cognitive distortions*—at the root of these thoughts. Maybe it's the unrealistic belief that you should always be happy or a catastrophic fear that setting limits with your parents will lead to withdrawal of their love and support. Are these thoughts true? Or are they just your perceived version of reality?

If the thoughts aren't accurate, practice replacing a guilty thought with a different one. This is called *thought restructuring*. Because it can be difficult to go from guilt straight into positivity, try a neutral thought first, such as, "Setting limits with my parents will be hard, but I can handle it." You can then work your way to a more positive thought if you'd like: "Setting limits with my parents will actually bring us closer, because we will understand one another better."

To summarize:

Become a nonjudgmental observer of your own thoughts.

Identify the thinking errors you may be making.

Practice a thought that is more neutral, or even positive, to replace the thinking error, even if you don't necessarily believe it yet.

Rinse and repeat, over and over.

This fourth step, repetition, is really important. Thought work is not a one-and-done substitution. You are literally rewiring your brain, practicing thoughts that at first may seem untrue or too positive, in order to create new pathways toward a less critical and more compassionate approach to yourself. The goal is to train your brain to respond with less guilt, and as with any goal, practice, in the form of time and effort, will allow you to reach the finish line.

Remember, because your brain has been jumping to these distorted thoughts repeatedly throughout your entire life, they may be so automatic, you don't even know they've occurred. You just know you're feeling guilty. Review the following list of the most common thinking errors—and we *all* have them—so you can better understand which ones might be present in your life. This will give you a powerful road map for taking action to lower your guilt.

1. **Catastrophizing:** Imagining the worst possible scenario, often involving quite an imaginative leap to a terrible outcome.

   Distorted Thought: "If I'm late for this meeting, I will definitely be fired, which means I will be unable to pay my rent and I will end up homeless, living under a bridge."

   Neutral Thought: "If I'm late, that will be frustrating, but I will just have to apologize and try to move on with my day."

Positive Thought: "This is not a big deal. I'm an important member of this team, and I know my work is good, so they won't even care if I'm running a little behind."

2. All-or-Nothing Thinking: Also known as black-and-white thinking, this kind of thought often has those extreme words we watch out for: *always, never, only.*

Distorted Thought: "I'll never reach my productivity goal unless I spend every hour working."

Neutral Thought: "No one can be available all the time. That's unfair."

Positive Thought: "Making time to rest and refuel is necessary and important, and I deserve to have some downtime. It will make me a more effective person."

3. Emotional Reasoning: I feel it, therefore it must be true.

Distorted Thought: "I feel lonely today. Nobody likes spending time with me because I'm boring."

Neutral Thought: "I feel lonely, which is hard. It won't last forever."

Positive Thought: "I feel a little lonely today, but that's human. It might even prompt me to reach out to my friend who I haven't seen in a while. What else can I do to care for myself right now?"

4. **"Should" Statements**: This is exactly what it sounds like. We have a thought that we "should" have done something, and if we didn't follow through, guilt can occur.

   Distorted Thought: "I should be calling my mother every day, because that's what a good daughter would do."

   Neutral Thought: "I haven't been calling my mother every day. That doesn't mean I don't love her."

   Positive Thought: "I'm a caring daughter, so of course I want to connect with my mom every day. I love having her in my life."

5. **Personalization**: We assume we are to blame for anything that goes wrong, accepting responsibility for areas far outside our control, just as we've been socialized to do. This includes our expectation that we can control the thoughts and feelings of others.

   Distorted Thought: "My daughter is in a terrible mood. I must have messed up something important."

   Neutral Thought: "My daughter is in a bad mood. It's difficult to see her that way."

   Positive Thought: "My daughter seems to be struggling with something. I know we have a good relationship, so she will talk to me if she needs support, and then I can try to encourage her."

You might use personalization in a variety of settings. Your spouse is irritable? They must be angry with you. Your boss expresses concern about yearly numbers? You assume they are referring specifically to your faltering productivity. Sometimes, you even use personalization in your interactions with perfect strangers. "When I walked by that woman on the street, she was frowning. She must think I look dumb in this new jacket."

Importantly, not only does this cognitive distortion increase feelings of guilt, it also prevents you from understanding what is *actually* going on with the other individual. Blaming yourself, you may become defensive, rather than remaining open for an important conversation, and you could miss what is really needed. Maybe your friend seems upset when you pick her up, which you assume is because you're running late. You start defending yourself with an excuse for your tardiness, so she has to interrupt you to tell you she just received some difficult news.

6. **Filtering**: Cancelling out all the positive thoughts or evidence and only paying attention to the negative.

Distorted Thought: "She just complimented me because she feels sorry for me. I could have done much more to prepare for this party."

Neutral Thought: "I'm seeing things about this party I would like to change."

Positive Thought: "I worked hard on this party and it has so many great features. Even if it's not perfect, I'm happy to hear that others are enjoying themselves."

As you consider these categories, there's no need to get too bogged down in the exact labels. Just know that these distortions shape our thoughts, and they are not accurate, helpful, or fair. Now, to put it all together, let's see how these different types of thoughts might have affected my client Andrea before a recent work event.

Andrea is a thirty-one-year-old single mom who recently moved to a new city for her job. Hoping to build a social network, she agreed to attend a cocktail hour with her colleagues. As she walked to the event, she could have had a variety of thoughts, from very negative to very positive.

Distorted Thought: "I never meet anyone at these things. I should be spending time with my daughter instead of going to this happy hour. I'm being so selfish."

Neutral Thought: "I may meet someone at this event. If not, I can always find other ways to connect. My daughter will probably be fine with the babysitter if I'm away for a couple of hours."

Positive Thought: "This could be so much fun! I usually love meeting new people. My daughter is also probably going to have a great time with her new babysitter tonight."

Reviewing these three versions of Andrea's thoughts, you can imagine how each might influence her mood and behavior. The first thought contains all-or-nothing thinking and a should statement and so may create feelings of sadness and frustration, possibly leading to self-defeating actions such as standing by herself at the event or even avoiding it altogether rather than risking expected rejection. The second, more neutral thought might help lower Andrea's anxiety about the event and help her feel motivated to speak to new people, even if it feels difficult, while the third thought could lead to excitement and an open and friendly attitude when she arrives. Importantly, they each also affect her level of guilt about being away from her daughter.

If you were Andrea, which outcome would you want? Which thoughts would help you get there?

Paying attention to the way our brain responds in certain situations involves effort, but it is so worth it. Yes, you may prefer that guilty thoughts didn't occur in the first place, but keep in mind, this is just your brain's way of trying to protect you. It wants to prepare you for any negative experiences. Remember the negativity bias, which skews us to focus on any potential threats or missteps rather than what has gone well? This ancient adaptation is no longer serving us, so if we want to live with agency instead of guilt, we must learn a different way.

This is not about glossing over everything with positivity. It's about encouraging your brain to assess situations with a less distorted, less pessimistic lens. Always responding to life with a worst-case mentality does not benefit us, and it's not even realistic. It's harmful. Instead, you can catch that automatic negative thought. Then—and this is really powerful—you can reject that thought in favor of a more accurate one.

For example, if Andrea notices she is stuck in the distorted thought, criticizing herself and feeling guilty for spending time away from her daughter, she can work on recognizing and validating the many amazing things she is doing each day in her various roles, rather than just brushing them aside. She might remind herself that this new job was offered to her because of her great work in her prior role, and that she is being a positive role model for her daughter by trying new things, even if she feels nervous. By practicing these shifts in her thinking, Andrea will notice it seems easier to come up with more encouraging thoughts. These reflections also help to bolster the "reality" portion of the Guilt Equation, with very positive results (and, as we hoped, much less guilt).

To summarize, your common thought errors might be the

first thing to pop into your mind, like a messy first draft, but they don't need to be the thoughts that you will *choose* to keep. Thoughts are *not* facts. Over time, finding more neutral or even positive replacements can help rewire your brain toward less guilt-provoking, automatic responses to life's stressors.

Nurturing a Growth Mindset

As you start to practice the thought-restructuring process, shifting from automatic negative and critical thoughts to more neutral or positive thoughts, you may run into a new challenge. It may seem very difficult to create these new types of thoughts out of the blue, without a clear framework. This is where learning about a growth mindset can be helpful.

Maybe you have been encouraged, at one time or another, to "nurture a growth mindset," but what exactly does that mean? Psychologist Dr. Carol Dweck, the author of *Mindset: The New Psychology of Success*, describes growth mindset as a belief that throughout our lives, we can strengthen aspects of ourselves, such as our skills and intelligence, with our efforts, choices, and help from others. In other words, we are all capable of positive growth.

The opposite of a growth mindset is a fixed mindset, or a belief in an unchangeable version of ourselves. Those with a fixed mindset believe their abilities are carved in stone—that they were born with only a certain amount of intelligence or talent, for example, and their job is to perpetually prove to others just how much of each of these characteristics they possess. But fear of failure is a stifling experience for creativity. It can also interfere with your ability to learn new skills, such as taking a different approach to guilt. The more you can emphasize that this process is about taking chances, falling down, and getting back up again, the more likely you are to move forward in your life with less guilt. In life, you either succeed or you learn. The only way to fail is by giving up entirely.

Let's begin by considering the key differences that set a growth mindset apart from a fixed mindset. A growth mindset encourages you to:[2]

Embrace challenges rather than avoid them.
Instead of immediately defaulting to guilty or critical thoughts, practicing a growth mindset suggests you lean into the difficult moment. Instead of "I'll never figure this out," tell yourself, "This is really difficult, but I know how to work hard, and I will find a way to get it done." Embracing challenging emotions—even difficult ones like guilt, grief, and sadness—is also part of a growth mindset. Avoidance can provide short-term relief, but it just allows the feelings to increase in strength, eventually showing up in unhelpful or destructive ways.

Persist in the face of setbacks, rather than get defensive or give up easily.

When you start paying attention to your guilty thoughts, you may feel frustrated by how often they emerge and how difficult it may feel to shift them. However, this shift is possible with persistence and curiosity. Instead of "I must be doing this wrong. Nothing is changing, so I should just quit," say, "I wish this were easier, but I know I'm moving in the right direction, and I can overcome roadblocks if I just keep trying."

View effort as the path to mastery rather than a waste of time.

A growth mindset encourages you to remind yourself you are spending time, energy, and attention on your thoughts and feelings with an important purpose. Lowering your excessive, draining guilt is not an effortless process, but it's worth it because you will emerge stronger, more joyful, and more engaged in your life. Instead of "I should have been able to fix this already. Clearly it's not working," say, "I'm proud of how hard I'm working, even though this is taking a long time, because I know my life is worth the effort."

Learn from criticism rather than ignore it.

Yes, you can learn from your critical thoughts. Having a growth mindset allows you to view your thoughts and feelings with curiosity, seeking to understand their patterns, triggers, even the sensations in your body when you have them. You can go from "I'm fine. I just need to get over this and move on" to "This conversation with my friend is really triggering guilt and some critical thoughts, even though I can't figure out what I might have done wrong. I must be running into an unfair expectation or ignoring my effort. Let me reflect on that for a moment."

Find lessons and inspiration in the success of others rather than feel threatened by their accomplishments.

Remember, it's human nature to compare yourself with others. As you do with your guilty thoughts, try to acknowledge feelings of envy toward another person with curiosity and compassion, because they are helpfully signaling your awareness of something you wish you had or believe you should have. Instead of "She just got an amazing promotion. I'll never be as successful as she is," say, "Wow, seeing her earn that promotion really affected me. I need to work hard and chase my dreams, too, because they're possible."

Keeping in mind these five features of a growth mindset, we can work on viewing our experiences—including setbacks—as part of a valuable process to lower excessive guilt, as well as a helpful outline for rewriting critical thoughts. You cannot change the past, nor can you use guilt to make up for missed opportunities or decisions you regret. However, by experimenting with aspects of a true growth mindset, you can see that any experience—even or *especially* the most difficult ones—can teach you crucial lessons about yourself and your values.

As you practice these tenets of a growth mindset in your own life, be on the lookout for a false growth mindset, such as "I just need to always stay positive. I should find the good in any situation and never feel guilty." Life brings painful losses, disappointments, and missed opportunities. If you try to force yourself to stay positive, you aren't validating or expressing your true feelings, which you now recognize is a crucial step in lowering your guilt and finding your agency. Instead, ask yourself questions that can help promote a growth mindset, such as "What did I get wrong today that taught me something?" or "What did I try hard at today?" You can also ask these kinds of questions with a group of important people in your life. "While we eat dinner, could we each share something we found difficult today? Then, let me ask you, do you think you learned anything from it?"

You can also practice mindful self-compassion by saying, "I know I'm feeling sad today, and that's understandable. This has been a difficult experience." Sometimes, when things go wrong, the only thing you can say is, "I've learned from this and I'm going to try again next time." Even when your mind tries to convince you that you can lessen the pain of a letdown with excessive worry, constant ruminating, or guilt, none of these will take away the sting of disappointment. You just have to face it, find the lesson, and do your best to move on.

Strategies from Positive Psychology

As we work on replacing guilt-ridden thoughts with neutral or even positive ones with help from a growth mindset, we can turn to another crucial practice for quieting guilt: filling our life with the positive. In other words, augmenting our perception of reality from "I'm not doing anything perfectly. My life is a mess," to "I'm really trying hard. My life isn't perfect, but it's filled with so many wonderful things." (Remember the Guilt Equation: Guilt = Expectations - Reality.)

This is a good time to introduce positive psychology, a field focused on the aspects of psychological health that help you flourish by highlighting the many things in your life that are going well.[3] There are five key areas of focus, all of which have been shown to increase your well-being when you give them time and attention. They can be remembered with the acronym PERMA.

Positive emotions

Engagement

Relationships

Meaning

Achievement

Each of the PERMA categories can help you begin to lessen your excessive guilt, either by setting more reasonable and achievable expectations for yourself or by bolstering positive aspects of your perceived reality, or maybe both! In this next section, you will learn how nurturing positive emotions, engagement, meaning, and achievement can all help you lower your toxic guilt. In the following chapter, you will also learn about strategies in your important relationships that can help you move away from guilt and toward a life with greater agency.

Positive Emotions

Nurturing positive emotions is a powerful tool for overcoming guilty thoughts. When you focus your attention on experiences you've enjoyed, you enrich and strengthen those memories, and you are more likely to evoke them in the future. This is certainly preferable to focusing on all the ways you are falling short, feeling guilty, and ruminating on setbacks or disappointments.

Cultivating positive emotions, much like preparing the soil before planting a flower garden, means creating a welcoming environment for growth. You can practice this by:

1. **Remembering a time you felt a positive emotion.** "I felt so proud when I finished that project, after hours of hard work! It was such an energizing feeling."

2. **Acting like you typically do when you feel a positive emotion.** "I started dancing in my living room, even though I felt tired, because I remembered how dancing usually makes me feel happy."

3. **Seeking out positive emotional situations.** "She seemed surprised when I came all the way over to her house to say thank you in person, but it felt so good to see her face when I gave her a card and a hug."

4. **Attending mindfully to how you feel when you are experiencing positive emotions.** In other words, if you are feeling good, take a moment to notice exactly what that feels like! "I'm so excited

to go see that new movie with my friends tonight. I feel a little jumpy inside and I notice I keep smiling."

5. Savoring the pleasure of a particular feeling or experience, which involves noticing and spending time appreciating positive experiences in your life.[4] "Remember when we rode on that roller coaster and took a ridiculous picture? The kids laughed so hard at us. It was really fun. I'm so glad we're finally all here together again. Let's try the giant water flume next! I think we're going to love it!"

Importantly, savoring can be utilized for events in the past, by *reminiscing*; in the present, when you *enjoy the moment*; and in the future, via *anticipation*. Or maybe you can do all of these at once!

Remember, even when you are practicing these strategies to try to increase your positive emotions, guilt may sneak in. "Yes, I feel proud, but I should have finished this project earlier," or "Dancing when I'm supposed to be doing the dishes! Why am I such a procrastinator?" This is why it's so important to recognize and address our guilty thoughts at the same time we are nurturing the positive, because, like food poisoning at a wedding reception, they can spoil even the happiest moments.

One positive psychology exercise that encourages you to remember positive experiences is called Three Good Things, which has been shown in research studies to significantly improve feelings of happiness. This exercise asks you to take a moment at the end of each day to write down three things that went well that day, as well as the cause of those things. These three things don't need to be anything momentous. In fact, sometimes it's the smallest successes that bring the most joy: "Today, I saw a beautiful cardinal at my bird feeder. I'm so glad I bought more birdseed!"

I also recommend trying Three Good Things in a group setting, such as with your family or at a gathering of friends. Not only do you share your positive moments out loud, focusing attention on this experience so you are more likely to remember it, you also will feel the pleasure and connection of hearing someone else's positive moments. When my family does this around the dinner table, my boys share tidbits of their day that would typically be lost in general statements about school being "fine." Maybe they did well on a quiz or they were proud of helping a classmate with a tricky math problem. I enjoy following up to learn more, because I hear about their positive experiences, which feels good, and I can note their evident pride when they answer my questions, so I know I'm also helping them remember these pleasant events.

Engagement

Engagement is the ability to use your skills, attention, and gifts optimally to meet a challenge. For example, you are working on a project for an upcoming presentation and are able to focus well, apply the necessary information you learned earlier, and meet the demands of the task. This aligns with the concept of *flow*, described by psychologist Mihaly Csikszentmihalyi as an optimal experience in which "thoughts, intentions, feelings, and all the senses are focused on the same goal. Experience is in harmony."[5] Engagement, or flow, then, is the opposite of disinterest, disengagement, and fractured attention, which can lead to burnout, exhaustion, and cynicism.

Putting time and energy into the endeavors that truly engage you is an important way to maintain a healthy and happy approach to your life. Not only does engagement feel good, it also improves your sense of self-efficacy and confidence to problem-solve. Therefore, one key way to help lower your guilt is to learn which jobs, roles, or experiences authentically draw your effort, enthusiasm, and pride. This self-knowledge, considered openly and with curiosity, allows you to set expectations for yourself that are fair, achievable, and aligned with these areas of true engagement.

This is especially important because guilt tends to arise when you set unfair expectations about the areas you believe you *should* find engaging. For example, do you limit your career interests to those you think are valuable to others, even if they don't light you up? This may cause you to set expectations for success or enjoyment in a job that will be very difficult to meet, worsening your guilt. Maybe you've told yourself the right thing to do is to get married and have children, so you'd better fall in line. If this isn't actually what you want to do, you are setting expectations of finding deep engagement as a wife and mother that you may not truly feel, and guilt will increase. Are you limiting your hobbies to those you think are most productive, when you'd love to try something new just for fun? If so, you are putting up roadblocks to engagement and creating guilt by feeling less than optimal pleasure in an activity you expect to enjoy. To nurture engagement, you must be aware of the barriers in your way, including an automatic dismissal of certain activities as frivolous or of lesser value. It's important to be aware of your expectations about "perfect" engagement, and to continue to allow an open exploration.

To find your own moments of true engagement, think back over the past several days and see if you can notice when time seemed to pass surprisingly quickly or when you were most energized. For example, were you cooking a meal and happily lost in the selection of tasty ingredients or were you putting together a new puzzle with intense concentration?

Keep in mind, something that is engaging for you doesn't

always have to bolster your productivity. Yes, it can enhance productivity if you are able to concentrate readily and work at length toward a particular goal, but this is not a necessary feature of engagement. It is not a failure if your most engaging moments don't align precisely with your responsibilities. After all, moments of amusement may not be "productive" per se, but they still may be the best, most memorable parts of your day. ("Can you believe I spent two hours on that paint-by-numbers picture last night? I was so focused, I didn't even realize how late it was! That was really fun.")

Meaning

You will learn strategies to support your important relationships in the next chapter. Here, as we consider the concept of meaning, I find one of the oldest definitions to be the most helpful. Aristotle described the term *eudaemonia*, which involves fostering one's best version of the self and using it to serve a greater good. He contrasted this with hedonism, or the singular pursuit of pleasure.[6]

For many of us, our choices about how to spend our time—whether in a career, as a volunteer, or as a parent—have become increasingly linked not only to our sense of achievement but also to our sense of purpose. You may be seeking eudaemonia in your roles both to demonstrate your productivity value to the outside world and to feed your need for deeper meaning. However, this can become almost paralyzing, as you search the existing opportunities for the perfect combination of passion, altruism, and worthiness of respect, not to mention practical considerations like salary and benefits. When you fail to find the ideal choice, your guilt steadily climbs as you become a victim of sky-high expectations, yet again.

I know women who have spent years searching for their identity within the ideal career, struggling when they felt a pull toward a variety of interests or skills. Placing particular careers on a hierarchy of value to society creates an unfair expectation of finding the "perfect" job, and it minimizes the contribution of women across the full spectrum of paid and unpaid work.

When you see examples, whether online or in your personal life, of people who seem to have absolute clarity about their life's passion, pursuing it with enviable, single-minded enthusiasm, you might feel lost, left behind, or guilty about your own missed opportunities. Your own authentic path can seem frustratingly opaque. However, remember that meaning can be found in a broad variety of places, whether it's in the traditional family recipe you cook for a holiday meal, the laughter you share with a colleague, the role you play in a community theater, or other ways you commit to living a life of empathy and gratitude, lowering your guilt in the process.

Achievement

Finally, we can begin to lower our guilt by reimagining our pursuit of achievement, which positive psychology suggests we need both extrinsically—such as a raise, an award, or other types of recognition—and intrinsically, in our own, internal sense of competence.

Rather than a feeling of accomplishment, guilt may arise when you review the choices you've made in your life and perceive lost opportunities or imperfect actions. For example, maybe your expectation reflects an idealized version of a steady climb toward the top of your organization. If you fail to reach this height, you blame yourself, believing you just didn't try hard enough. By taking full responsibility for your life trajectory, you are again trying to take responsibility for factors that exist far outside your locus of control. I'm not saying you need to blame others for missteps or missed opportunities, but consider what it might feel like to shift your emotion from guilt, based on the belief that it was all in your control and you messed up, to one of frustration and determination, working against the *problem* rather than against yourself.

It is also important to be careful so external goals and validation don't become your primary focus, at the expense of other areas of your life—one, because they contain so many variables outside your control, and two, because they are unpredictable in their benefit for your overall happiness. Indeed, sometimes, even if you believe you have found the ideal job or role, problems can occur when you realize these achievements don't bring you as much joy or other positive emotions as you expected. You may also lose touch with your deeper purpose, feeling disconnected and unsure how to seek out meaning in other areas of your life.

What would it be like to shift your focus to intrinsic achievements, meaning the areas of competence that you appreciate in yourself? Maybe you struggle to even begin this exploration, telling yourself, "I have no idea what I'm good at." Another positive psychology exercise, called Using Signature Strengths in a New Way, can help you in this quest to understand yourself and nurture your strengths.

To begin this exercise, identify your specific strengths in the VIA Survey of Character Strengths, an evidence-based questionnaire created through significant research (authentichappi ness.sas.upenn.edu/home).[7] These signature strengths fall into six main categories: wisdom/knowledge, courage, transcendence, humanity, justice, and temperance. Some examples of signature strengths include humor and playfulness, love of learning, fairness, humility, and open-mindedness.

After learning your top five signature strengths, research suggests you will feel happier if you make a point to use these strengths in a new way every day for at least one week. For example, if one of your signature strengths is "love of learning," consider reading one article about a different subject each day; if it's "creativity," maybe find some inexpensive supplies at a local craft store and try making something new every morning. People who tried this strategy for just seven days described improved happiness lasting as long as six months. Think how well it could work if you kept trying these strengths on a regular basis, not to mention the likely positive effects on those around you.

Though it's true that we all need positive feedback and validation for our efforts, much of the work recommended in this book is about shifting from seeking external achievement to an internal sense of your value, competency, and dedication. Indeed, holding a loving and supportive view of yourself may be the most important accomplishment of all, creating an unmovable force against life's many trials.

There are three key principles I've learned in helping women break free from excessive guilt around achievement:

1. **The need to always feel special or to see yourself as something held apart from others due to some achievement at work, in your relationships, even with your children, keeps you trapped in a never-ending cycle of striving and fearfully avoiding failure.** The expectations rise, your perception of yourself stays still or even wors-

ens, and the guilt continues to grow. If, instead, you can focus on the things you are doing well, the signature strengths you are expressing, and the growth you are demonstrating, the guilt can begin to lessen.

Here's another important point to consider: If you choose not to gauge your life by the traditional model of how high you can rise above others, you can design and implement another strategy for measurement, one that assesses how high you can rise *with* others. Could you balance the overwhelming focus on being "better" than others with the desire to be *part of* something better? It's powerful to recognize the potential of your deep desire to connect and collaborate, and the sense of achievement this could deliver.

2. **The guilt will lessen when you relinquish the idea of what a "perfect" woman should achieve.** Your education and experiences, along with the awareness of the human condition they've provided, can be utilized in novel ways best aligned with your gifts, with positive results. You can be the best version of yourself, accepting your flaws and supporting yourself toward a life with more agency.

3. **You are allowed to limit, without guilt, roles and environments that you find harmful to your health and well-being.** This is true no matter what others believe you should be doing or what goals you've previously set for yourself. Period.

Don't downplay the many remarkable things you achieve each and every day. Remember, you have the final say in what it means to live a happy, successful life.

❋

Working on lowering guilty thoughts and feelings, as well as nurturing positive emotions, engagement, meaning, and achievement, all take practice, just like regular exercise. You must continue to do the work, because those who continue to practice these exercises—Three Good Things and Using Signature Strengths in a New Way—are more likely to report improvements in their happiness and lower levels of depression over time. Fortunately, lowering your guilt will also play a powerful role in this joyful revolution.

Now, let's shift gears to consider additional actions you can take to lower your guilt, particularly in your interactions with your loved ones and the outside world. As social creatures, very few of us thrive in isolation. Though you cannot change the thoughts and feelings of others, you can learn how to engage differently with these individuals, effecting positive change through clear communication of your authentic agency.

7.

Engaging with Agency

As we've learned so far, one of the most insidious sources of excessive guilt is the tendency—born out of and reinforced via socialization—for women to take responsibility for things and people outside our control. We are encouraged to prioritize others' feelings above our own, and to view ourselves as failures if we cannot play each of our many roles perfectly, while keeping everyone happy. Therefore, lowering your excessive guilt—and particularly your unreachable expectations—requires you to be *very clear* about the current ways you interact with others, and to consider which of these you want to keep doing, and which ones you will choose to set aside.

In this chapter, we will continue to take action by learning how to set helpful boundaries, practice delegation, and accept the presence of disappointment, both in yourself and in others. First, though, let's discuss the importance of having a strong, supportive social network as you take these actions in your life, and how nurturing your important relationships, especially through a powerful new way of communicating in them, will bolster you on your path to less guilt.

Mobilizing Social Support

One of the most vital actions you can take to lower your guilt is to nurture your most important relationships. Remember, you, like many remarkable women, are doing remarkable things. You may also be asking yourself to be the perfect mother, wife, daughter, partner, employee, and friend. Please allow yourself to also be *human*, and remember that as a human, you need people in your life to nurture a deep sense of belonging and resilience.

Sometimes, you may take your loved ones for granted, seeing them as stable forces while you try to "improve" yourself or an aspect of your life. However, research—and intuition, I think—predicts you will be happiest when you do your very best to nurture these important social connections. This is also why the final focus in positive psychology you will learn is the development of positive relationships.

Loneliness is not only difficult emotionally, it also has negative consequences for your health.[1] You are a social being; therefore, you rely on those in your emotional orbit for a significant portion of your health and happiness. Nowhere is this more visible than in the potential for heightened guilt during times of significant interpersonal change, including major life transitions like marriage, retirement, relationship conflicts, and losses of those people most important to us.[2] These events can put a strain on your connections with loved ones as you all try to cope with the stress of disruption. In these moments, communication is crucial to lowering your guilt, because it will allow you to advocate for the things you need, as well as those you want, and help you build a stronger sense of agency while still nurturing closeness with others. Your personal safety net of important people is crucial for weathering the storm of various life stressors and pushing back against the harmful expectations these periods can create.

You can identify who makes up your personal safety net by conducting what's called an interpersonal inventory. After drawing three concentric circles on a blank piece of paper, fill in the names of those in your orbit, with the outside circle for acquaintances and other casual connections; the middle circle for closer friends, family, and other more meaningful relationships; and the inner circle for the people you most deeply love and trust, often those you would first confide in after a major life event, good or bad.

If it seems like your inner circle is more limited than you'd like, try to identify individuals who share your values and, most important, are willing to be real about their own challenges and missteps. That's the difference between being met with empathy and validation ("Oh my gosh, I had the same argument with my daughter last week! She swears she's wearing shorts under that long T-shirt, but you can't see them at all.") and apathy and judgment ("You had an argument with your daughter? You shouldn't lose your cool like that.").

Do Social Media Friends Count?

Short answer? It depends.

You would probably agree that social media has some downsides, to put it mildly. It has been suggested that it's a major contributor to rising rates of loneliness, anxiety, and depression, particularly in children and adolescents. However, viewing social media with an all-or-nothing lens is also not helpful. Similar to television or certain foods, it might be the way you *consume* social media that matters most. Short of unplugging completely—which is certainly a reasonable choice if it makes sense for you—consider using social media in a different way.

For example, I came across a recent paper on the use of social media among women physicians.[3] Assuming I would read about the anxiety-inducing comparisons and toxic discourse online, I was surprised by some of the positive effects of social media discussed there.

1. Many women express encountering challenges in accessing the mentorship and networking necessary for promotion to leadership roles. Social media may actually help us make important networking and mentorship connections in far-reaching ways, unlimited by geographical location or introductions from current—often male—institutional leaders.

2. Social media is "open" 24-7, so even if you have an erratic schedule, you can seek support when you have time and availability.

3. Private online groups may provide a (relatively) safe space to discuss sexual harassment, parenting stressors, relationship conflicts, workplace discrimination, and other sensitive topics.

4. Even if you struggle with self-promotion, social media allows you to share your knowledge in new and more visible ways, which can also lead to positive collaboration and further opportunities.

5. I think this one is the most important: Advocacy for change can be created by the power of a coordinated group of like-minded women working toward a common goal.

To summarize, social media *can* provide benefits, particularly for those who may lack a voice within more traditional channels of influence. Yes, there are very problematic aspects of social media, which should not be underestimated. However, I share this study to suggest women consider the potential benefits in finding mentorship, access, support, validation, and a powerful community of compassionate and engaged peers through creative avenues. Maybe we can work together to find something better than social media to reach these goals, so we can help one another build our powerful sense of agency.

The Gratitude Visit is another positive psychology exercise that can help you emphasize your connection with others. Think of someone still alive who did something that made a positive difference in your life. When you have that person in mind, write them a letter describing the powerful effect they had on you and how you continue to benefit from their influence. Then, crucially, *reach out* to that person to share this letter with them. Not only does this make the other person feel valued, it can also improve your own happiness.

As you try to nurture your important relationships, you may notice you get stuck in certain communication ruts, which often contain the same types of words common in triggering excessive guilt. *Should, always,* and *never* are overgeneralizations you may assume about others, but just as these cognitive distortions limit your self-confidence, they can also harm your important relationships. Additionally, watch out for those moments when guilt interferes with your willingness to reach out for support. You might tell yourself, "I can't tell my friend about these migraines I've been having. She'll just worry about me even more. I'll call her when I'm feeling better." Maybe you try to take on this protective role toward your loved ones, believing you will be "too much" for them.

However, this is another important time to evaluate your expectations and perceptions of reality. Are you expecting yourself to be without pain or disappointment, so you never "burden" your friends and family? Are you also overlooking the many times you've been able to support the people in your life, even when it's difficult, because that's what connection means?

As you try to express your own thoughts and feelings, you can also practice a curious, nonjudgmental stance toward your loved one. Notice how this mirrors your approach toward your own thoughts. For example, rather than assuming your partner will say no to helping you with a project, you can gather the courage to actually ask them, without expecting the worst. Instead of believing your family member will make an invalidating statement like "You just need to get over that," you can continue to try sharing your authentic feelings. True, this doesn't always lead to the desired change, because the other person is allowed to make their own decisions and assessments. However, it has the powerful *potential* to reshape your interactions.

By keeping an eye on your unreasonable expectations in your relationships, you can work with your partner to bridge communication gaps and design the best path forward. Sharing your experiences, recognizing when you may be expecting mind reading or when you may be letting guilt dictate your decisions, you can work to shift these unhelpful approaches. You also must nurture hope that the communication, even if it's uncomfortable or awkward, can bring you to a new level of intimacy and support in your relationships, not to mention a lot less of that painful, excessive guilt.

As you begin to lower the unfair expectations and self-criticism leading to excessive guilt, those in your emotional orbit—friends, family, colleagues—are likely to notice a change, and they will have their own feelings about your new approach. With this in mind, it is particularly important for you to communicate clearly during this transitional time, rather than letting others guess what you might be thinking or feeling. This is where boundaries become so important.

Setting Boundaries

Boundaries—the limits and rules you set regarding your interactions with others—guide how you share many important aspects of yourself, particularly your time, emotional energy, and effort. By setting a clear boundary with another person, you are communicating: (1) I matter to myself enough to protect my time, energy, and effort, (2) here are the expectations I've set for myself, and finally, (3) ignoring this boundary, or pushing your own expectations on me, will not likely have the effect you are seeking.

For example, setting a boundary at work with a statement like, "I will respond to your email within two business days," means you value your time enough to set a reasonable response expectation, you are voicing this expectation clearly, and those who may want a response more quickly will, ideally, adjust their own expectations. Now, this doesn't mean boundaries will allow you to control someone else's response, any more than guilt could, but you are giving yourself the best chance at being heard and understood.

If boundaries are completely absent, leaving you wide open to the requests and expectations of others to share all your time, energy, and effort, this is not only draining but can lead to resentment, anger, even depression. It also means you're basing your expectations on the needs of others, letting their lives take precedent. Additionally, zero boundaries often leaves you with little left for the activities and people you truly value, including yourself.

Boundaries, then, are the scaffolding you will use to create room for a life with agency rather than guilt. You are protecting yourself from an expectation of constant caretaking, responsibility for other people's emotions, attempts to reach perfection, and a perfectly balanced life. You are creating the possibility of your reality matching your expectations, in a way that is clearly communicated to the people in your life.

Several challenges may arise as you begin setting clear boundaries. First, there is no handbook outlining your unique limits and rules, so you must choose them for yourself, in each situation. You may love being available for a late-night call from your daughter while she's away at college, but you tell your friend you'd prefer that she call you in the afternoon if she wants to chat.

Also, these decisions about your boundaries must be repeatedly revised, because as you grow and change, your boundaries may need to be adjusted. For example, before you had children you might have been happy to join your partner on a spontaneous weekend away, but now you let him or her know you would need several weeks' notice to plan this kind of trip. Once you accept that you cannot be all things to all people—such as a spontaneous weekend traveler—you can begin to make decisions about your most important boundaries. For example, you may decide to reprioritize where you spend your time or who you allow into your inner emotional circle. The self-knowledge you've gained during the earlier sections of the book provides a crucial road map for setting limits, because you recognize where your expectations may be unfairly high or over-influenced by the opinions of others.

Boundaries are also crucial in your work life. Maybe you've spent years building expertise in your career and enjoy the identity provided by your professional role. However, you realize you're currently miserable in the actual day-to-day work. You may decide to shift the boundaries you've set on your time and effort, stepping back from taking on extra projects, for example, in order to make room for your personal life or other desired pursuits.

Guess what you will probably feel, at least at first, when you try to set boundaries based on your *own* needs and goals.

Here's a hint: It starts with *G* and rhymes with *built*.

So much guilt can emerge when you set boundaries, because making changes risks disappointment—both your own and others'—and feelings of loss. Maybe you're asking your partner to stop criticizing your friends after you spend time together or trying to tell your parents you don't agree with the way they're disciplining your children. New boundaries require new, often difficult conversations, and you can only control one person in this setting: yourself!

You may also notice you miss some aspects of your life you experienced before setting a more sustaining boundary. Maybe you've always enjoyed being the one your friends turned to when they needed an ear, but you've realized you can't always be available. However, when you start setting limits to have time and energy for your family, you miss those intimate inter-actions with your friends. Or maybe you took pride in being the person at work who would always agree to the last-minute proj-ect or extra shift, but now that you've been saying no more of-ten to protect yourself from burnout, you miss having the reputation for taking on everything.

Though these feelings of loss or disappointment may be painful, you know you can tolerate them, and that the discom-fort will lessen with time and consistency. You also recognize the many benefits of learning to set reasonable boundaries in your life, including a decrease in your painful guilt.

Here are some key things to remember to help you set appropriate boundaries:

> Recognize that boundaries are necessary for your health and the strength of your relationships, as well as your goal of living with less guilt.

> Look inward to understand what you truly need and desire in your life and in your interactions with others.

> Speak up with clear, calm, and consistent communication.

> Adjust your boundaries as you grow and change, restarting and traveling through the whole process again.

> Expect that others will have feelings about your boundaries, such as anger, confusion, or disappointment.

That last one can feel really overwhelming. When you are asking for a shift in previously accepted dynamics with other people, they will have feelings about this and may share them quite forcefully, even if it's in the form of the silent treatment. If you expect to be able to protect others from difficult emotions—which you now know is impossible—this unrealistic expectation will just lead to even more guilt.

Yes, you will eventually set limits others don't like or maybe believe are unfair or disruptive, and it can be difficult to stand behind them. The emotional experiences of others can really challenge your belief that your needs and desires are important enough to create these waves. However, my response to that conflict involves returning to an earlier point: You are *important*. Your feelings are important. Creating boundaries to protect your precious life is so, so important. Please don't give them up.

Now, after validating your very normal and healthy need for adequate boundaries, let's discuss how you can cope with one of the most difficult responses you may receive when you set these limits: disappointment.

Allowing Disappointment

Being a woman today creates a nearly impossible setting for someone who hates to disappoint. Every day you have to say things like, "No, I can't do that for you right now," because you cannot possibly say yes to every request or demand on your time. However, you may still try.

When you arrive at a difficult decision point, recognizing your human limitations, you may decide the best course of action is to disappoint *yourself*, particularly if you believe that by this action you can absorb the pain or frustration of your loved ones. You say yes to activities you dislike or even hate, rather than asserting your true interests and needs, because you want to make other people happy. You turn down opportunities to enjoy time alone, fearing you will create disappointment in your family or friends. You repeatedly sacrifice your desires and goals because they may interfere with the needs of others.

In your attempts to avoid disappointing others, you may bend over backward and place yourself in unsustainable positions. Not only will this likely fail, it can cause problems in your important relationships. For example, trying not to disappoint a parent may lead to conflict with your spouse. *You simply cannot please everyone, all the time.*

You've been socialized to place yourself last on the priority list, disappointing yourself before all others, to avoid feeling guilty. Consider the cost of this behavior, however. Not only are you feeling disappointed, you're also probably suffering from a ton of guilt anyway. Furthermore, if you are a role model for important people in your life, such as your friends or your children, you are also teaching them to place themselves last. Lastly, by trying to protect others from feeling disappointment, you are also preventing them from learning an important lesson: Disappointment is a *normal* part of life.

You may have such a strong reaction to the disappointment of others that you try to immediately fix it, so you don't feel so guilty. Maybe you tell your son he can't go to a friend's house but then cancel your own plans to take him to his favorite store. Or maybe you have to cancel lunch with your parents at the last minute and, sensing their disappointment, agree to spend the weekend with them even though you have other plans. You can see how fearing the disappointment of others can lead you to make decisions that don't actually serve you.

Instead, you can learn to expect that if you are a human living in modern society, you will inevitably have to disappoint people sometimes. Remember, you can't be everything to everyone. The goal is to de-catastrophize disappointment. It isn't truly harmful, and it won't last forever. Instead of responding to your son's disappointment with frantic action, consider saying to him, "I know this is disappointing. I'm sorry the timing doesn't work out today." Then—and this can be difficult—you just let him share his feelings, without trying to fix them. Or when you have to cancel a lunch with your parents, you say, "I'm really sorry I can't make it for lunch today as we had planned. I know that's disappointing." You've communicated that you understand how they might be feeling, and you're sorry, but you don't have to immediately try to fix their emotions by offering something you may not be able to give.

Try to remember these key ideas to help de-catastrophize disappointment and limit additional guilt:

Your friends and family will survive feelings of disappointment, even if they seem very upset. They will not feel that way forever.

You can be a loving person and still accept that your choices may cause others disappointment.

Saying no can still be the correct choice, even if it disappoints someone you care about.

The responsibilities you carry bring with them the burden of your loved ones' potential dissatisfaction. It takes great patience and self-confidence to repeatedly clarify your boundaries, especially if this involves turning down your loved ones' requests. You must continue to remind yourself that you are still a caring person, even when you say no.

It's also important to learn how to tolerate your own disappointment. Rather than trying to escape this feeling the moment it emerges, you can allow yourself to experience it. "I wish I hadn't missed that dinner with my friends. It sounds like they had a blast." It's important to try to sit with it for a moment. Notice how it feels in your body. Yes, it might be really uncomfortable, especially when you first start making this shift, but over time, repetition will lessen the intensity. You will also learn that it doesn't automatically lead to a terrible outcome. You can recognize that disappointment, like any emotion, will not last forever, and this temporary nature of disappointment is the same when others are experiencing it. In fact, they, too, can learn to accept the feeling and recognize it will eventually pass, even though it may really hurt in the moment.

Remember, disappointment, much like guilt, can be an adaptive emotion. It works best when it highlights something you wish you had experienced or perhaps done differently, and you are able to make an alternative choice in the future. However, you will benefit enormously if you don't see it as something damaging you should avoid at all costs. Instead, you can learn to live with some disappointment, in yourself as well as in others, because it is absolutely normal.

Now that we've learned about the necessity of healthy boundaries and allowing disappointment, what's next? The power of delegation.

Delegating

Delegation is simply shifting a task from yourself to someone else. This is a skill that, done well, is the mark of a talented leader. It can not only lessen your extensive to-do list but can also empower the other people in your life to learn and grow by trying something new. But how can delegation help you lower your guilt?

Remember, you have been socialized to take on so many responsibilities—constant caretaking, managing other people's emotions, demonstrating balance—with perfect ease and competency. Think of delegation as one of the ways to push back on this socialization. By practicing the art of asking others to take on responsibility, you can reset your outsize expectations from doing it all to something far more manageable. Plus, if you aren't expecting the impossible of yourself, you will be less likely to view your efforts as just not enough. Delegation, then, shifts the variables of the Guilt Equation in a helpful and sustaining way, lowering your guilt in the process.

The ability to delegate tasks can be a challenging one, but it can be learned. It's understandable to take pride in the roles you play in your family, relationships, and career, and you may have difficulty relinquishing your identity as the hardest-working or most competent member in the room. There will certainly be bumps along the road, not to mention guilt, as you step back from trying to take care of everyone and everything.

However, living with less guilt and more agency is *worth the effort*. Finding ways to share responsibility while surviving the discomfort and self-doubt that may emerge can open you up to new opportunities. Over time, other people, whether they are your partner, children, friends, or colleagues, will learn to adjust to this new baseline, rather than assuming you will take on *every* task.

Think about whether you currently use delegation in your life. If you are home with a family member and notice there are many tasks that need to be done, how often do you ask those around you for help? What about in a work environment? Do you notice differences in the guilt produced by delegation, depending on the setting? Practicing delegation may feel harder in some areas of your life than others, which can be a helpful guide to tell you where you might want to focus some time and attention on this helpful skill.

If you are patient and persistent, others will begin stepping into those vacated roles. Keep in mind, perfectionism can be a problem here, too. If others are willing and able to take on some of these tasks, you must let them, even if you think they will mess it up. Asking for help and then criticizing someone else's approach will most certainly backfire in the long run. For example, when my husband remakes the bed after I've done a perfectly acceptable, B+ job, I tell him he will be making it on his own for the foreseeable future.

If perfection is impossible even when *you* take on the task, then let's learn to accept the imperfection created by others as well. You must learn to let go of the ideal, and instead work on accepting "good enough." Over time, this will seem less fraught, and you will learn you don't have to manage everything, minute by minute.

Another important tool is knowing what you can ignore

when you delegate. If you ask someone to take on a task, see if you can purposely "miss" the tone of their response, focusing instead on the actions your request brings. For example, if you ask your partner to help you clean out the basement, they are allowed to have their own feelings about it, and even to express them. However, if they sigh loudly and then say, "Fine, I guess," with irritation, see if you can focus on the words and ignore the tone. "Thank you!" will be the only necessary reply.

Yes, you may feel guilty when you start asking others to take on responsibilities you've previously held. You may worry about how this change will be perceived by others. "Will they think I'm lazy?" Honestly, you may also face a great deal of judgment from yourself. These kinds of self-critical thoughts are not unexpected. Yes, they are a barrier to change, because they cause discomfort. However, you can continue to practice reasonable delegation *even though* it creates these feelings. Guilt is no longer in control, and you are choosing to set limits on your time and energy, knowing you can find something better on the other side of hyper-competence and exhaustion.

Keep Going

Like so many things in life, from self-esteem to communication in our relationships, it will take time, patience, and *lots* of practice to make and maintain improvements in your relationship with guilt. However, I wrote this book to show you how, and I *know* you can do it.

As you reach the final step in the SPEAK process, I hope you feel empowered to try some of these recommendations in your daily life. Women, we are warriors. However you look at it, being a modern woman is *hard*, and continuing to try each day is an unbelievable accomplishment. Navigating this life can be so much easier if you aren't also burdened by excessive guilt.

Conclusion

Beginning to live with less guilt will transform your life in powerful ways. You will show up differently in your relationships with your loved ones, including being more open about the areas where you may be struggling, better able to set fair and reasonable boundaries, and willing to tolerate difficult feelings in others, including disappointment. You will begin asking for things you need, without punishing yourself for relying on others instead of doing everything yourself. You will apply the art of delegation with people in your life, including your family, friends, and colleagues, ignoring their bluster and complaints and simply saying thank you when they agree to take on a task or responsibility. You will treat yourself with compassion when you feel overwhelmed, frustrated, or just too damn tired to get everything done, recognizing this is simply you being human.

Instead of distracting yourself with guilt, you will allow yourself to feel sadness when you see changes in your loved ones and you will recognize your limitations in controlling their moods and always being available to care for them. You will be able to remain by their side as they share their fears, difficult emotions, and challenges, listening and loving, without taking responsibility or trying to "fix" their pain.

Most powerfully, you will be able to respond to your own critical voice with curiosity and compassion far more often than with self-criticism and judgment. When you recognize the voice of guilt asking if you really deserve rest or fun or even the freedom to say no to expectations about what a "perfect" woman should do, you will remind this voice, again and again, that you absolutely do. You will remember to tell yourself every day that you have value just as you *are*, not because of anything you *do*.

You can't expect yourself to immediately and completely switch over to compassionate curiosity. True change takes time. Yes, guilt will continue to emerge in your day-to-day life, but this is not failure. It's human. Importantly, though, now that you know how to investigate your expectations and perceptions of reality with the Guilt Equation, you can show up differently. Guilt will no longer be in control, having been replaced by your powerful and authentic sense of agency.

Conclusion

Women can do absolutely anything we set our minds to do. What you need to do next is let go of the belief that *all of it* is still your job. You are working through your own adaptations, and it is challenging, for sure. However, if you could do it with self-control and guilt alone, you'd be there already. Instead, we have to forge a new path.

As you begin to engage with the world in a different way, you must not underestimate the effect you may have on other women. It can be difficult to make the changes you are learning about here, but finding women who are working on their own relationship with toxic guilt can help you stay motivated and energized. You will also be part of a growing movement of women who refuse to reinforce these unfair expectations in one another, modeling, instead, a life lived with agency and empowerment. You will certainly not be alone.

As the balance of expectations moves toward a tipping point, eventually we will cascade into the vision of the future I hold for each of us: proud of our accomplishments, self-compassionate in our very human limitations and failures, and able to love intensely, without assuming responsibility for others' choices and experiences. I'm absolutely thrilled to partner with you on this journey.

Indeed, you are *already* enough, and you deserve to live guilt free.

Acknowledgments

This book is all about setting reasonable expectations, but trying to thank everyone who has contributed to my work is truly an impossible goal. I have been the fortunate recipient of decades of wonderful teachers, amazing friends, and a loving and supportive family, and they're all present in my writing. I will try to highlight many of them here, and I hope I can continue to share my thanks beyond these limited pages.

To begin, I realize I would still be using search prompts like "How Do I Actually Publish a Book?" if I hadn't connected with my wonderful agent, Sophie Cudd, at The Book Group. Thank you, Sophie, for taking a chance on a new writer and for answering my many questions with enthusiasm, professionalism, and patience. It is still a wonder to have you on my side, helping me navigate this new and thrilling terrain with your expertise.

Another incredibly fortunate connection I made was with Nina Rodríguez-Marty, my editor at Penguin Life. Nina, you took the raw material of my written musings and shaped it into something miraculous: a coherent and thoughtful book. It was an absolute delight to receive your thorough and creative edits and recognize your commitment to helping me dig deeper and clarify further. You are a truly gifted editor.

I want to offer additional thanks to Jennifer Houghton for your guidance in this process, with your crystal-clear communications and keen understanding about what information I most needed. I referred back to your emails repeatedly and always found the answers I sought. In addition, Jenny Meyer, my foreign rights agent, thank you for spreading the word about my book far beyond the US, and for your patience and enthusiasm with each new possibility.

An enormous thank you to my publisher at Viking Penguin, Brian Tart. It is an honor to be part of your roster of authors, many of whom have inspired me greatly in my personal and professional life. I also want to express my deep thanks to Meg Leder, the Penguin Life editorial director and a friendly face from our first meeting. You generously welcomed me into the Penguin Life family, and I will always be grateful for your confidence in my work. Additionally, thank you to the team at Sheldon Press, including Victoria Roddam, for partnering with me to share the book throughout the UK. I'm delighted to be working with you.

When I began this journey, I didn't realize how many diligent individuals contributed to the creation of the books I love. I want to offer a heartfelt thank you to those at Penguin, including managing editor Nick Michal, production editor Megan Gerrity, marketer Raven Ross, publicist Shelby Meizlik, and jacket designer Dave Litman.

I wouldn't be where I am today without the professors and mentors I had throughout my medical training at Columbia and UCLA, and my dear friends and colleagues at Penn. I've learned an incredible amount from so many brilliant teachers.

A big thank you to the amazing women at Introspective Spaces, Anu Gorukanti and Laura Holford, and my Artist's Way group—Amna, Ana, Leanne, and Ashley—for cheering me on as a writer and amateur crafter. Our weekly meetings gave me such a boost of confidence and encouragement when I needed it most.

Dr. Tracy Levitt, thank you for your guidance, support, and encouragement as I've made this pivot in my life. You helped me find my way when I felt so stuck, and you encouraged my desire to write when I needed it most. I've learned so much from working with you.

It is a joy to have so many compassionate, hilarious, supportive friends traveling through adulthood with me. Megan Breaks, thank you for reading a very early draft and providing a generous "vibe check." Your feedback was so welcome in this long process! Leslie Assini, thank you for inspiring me with your wonderful books and the joy you reflect when you are reading aloud to children. I'm so glad Sutton Terrace brought us together.

Acknowledgments

My dear friend, Dr. Kristin Leight. I'm so thrilled we started at Penn together. You've taught me an incredible amount about how to be a mother, a therapist, and a friend. Thank you for encouraging me through my many ups and downs, and I can't wait for our next dinner date. You are such a gift in my life.

The fabulous Lauren Grodstein, thank you for being the best damn neighbor/friend/brilliant writer/motivational speaker I could ask for. Thank you for your guidance, feedback, and all-around excellence. Come find me on my porch for a glass of wine.

John Kelleher, my dear friend and favorite performance partner. No one can belly laugh like you. I miss you so much. I hope you can see me trying to live with just a touch of your creative energy.

Lynn and Derek Reid, thank you for welcoming me into your wonderful family with open arms. It has been an honor to spend these years with you, learning from your generosity and your commitment to family. Your son has been shaped by such wonderful people.

To the sisters I've gained throughout my life, Kelly, Kim, and Brittany, thank you for teaching me so much about how to be a modern woman. You are each so brilliant, accomplished, and incredibly kind. I'm lucky to have you just a phone call away.

Grandma Grossman, thank you for inspiring me with your life as an educator and librarian. There is still no place I'd rather be than wandering the aisles of my local library, and I know you are smiling down on me as I explore the shelves for my next treasure.

Grandma Jacobson, thank you for teaching me how to speak up for what I believe in and have the courage to take an unexpected path. You were always willing to tell me just one more story, read me one more book, or make just one more delicious batch of homemade donuts.

My brother, Josh, thank you for being my first best friend and a fellow book lover and writer. Every time we hang out, you teach me something fascinating and make me laugh. Also, thank you for letting me play with your friends when we were growing up, even when I was really annoying.

My sister, Jodi, thank you for being my guilt muse. Just kidding. But not really. Thank you for helping me find the humor during the toughest times. You're my first call when I'm losing it, and you always find a way to help me feel better. Please say hello to the chickens and donkeys for me.

Thank you, Dad, for letting me find my own way, even when the path didn't always align with yours. It is an honor to share the profession of medicine with you, and I never tire of hearing you say you're proud of me. We've always just understood each other, haven't we?

Thank you, Mom, for your role as my head cheerleader, joy magnifier, and inspiring model for motherhood. Thank you for teaching me not to take myself so seriously, and for volunteering to be my one-woman marketing team. I will make sure all of your tennis and animal-shelter friends have a signed copy. Now we've both written a book!

To my son Sander, who lives his life one-handed, because he is always holding a book in the other. Your curiosity and wisdom inspire me, and I learn something new from you every day. I can't wait to watch you find your inspiration in this wide world.

To my son Callum, who promised to read my book "from front to cover." I love that sparkle in your eye, even when you're teasing me. Your creativity and enthusiasm are contagious, and I know you will continue to explore the world fearlessly.

To Jem, my sounding board and best friend, thank you for laughing at my jokes and taking my writing dreams seriously. You've always had the ability to soothe my nerves and fill me with confidence, even when you remake the bed as soon as I leave the room. Your commitment to our family is lovely to behold, and I am truly a lucky woman to spend my life with you.

Finally, to the thousands of patients who've shared their lives and stories with me over the years, teaching me something with each discussion. I'm so grateful for your patience and trust, exploring your lives in my office with courage and grace. It has been an honor to care for you.

Notes

Chapter 1: Understanding Guilt

1 Amrisha Vaish, "The Prosocial Functions of Early Social Emotions: The Case of Guilt," *Current Opinion in Psychology* 20 (April 2018): 25–29, https://doi.org/10.1016/j.copsyc.2017.08.008.

2 Roy Baumeister et al., "Guilt: An Interpersonal Approach," *Psychological Bulletin* 115, no. 2 (1994): 243–67, https://doi.org/10.1037/0033-2909.115.2.243.

3 Robert Plutchik, "A Psychoevolutionary Theory of Emotions," *Social Science Information* 21, nos. 4–5 (1982): 529–53, https://doi.org/10.1177/053901882021004003.

4 June Price Tangney et al., "Moral Emotions and Moral Behavior," *Annual Review of Psychology* 58 (January 2007): 345–72, https://doi.org/10.1146/annurev.psych.56.091103.070145.

Chapter 2: Why Do Women Experience So Much Guilt?

1 Linda Torstveit et al., "Empathy, Guilt Proneness, and Gender: Relative Contributions to Prosocial Behavior," *Europe's Journal of Psychology* 12, no. 2 (2016): 260–70, https://doi.org/10.5964/ejop.v12i2.1097.

2 Tamara Ferguson and Heidi Eyre, "Engendering Gender Differences in Shame and Guilt: Stereotypes, Socialization, and Situational Pressures," in *Gender and Emotion: Social Psychological Perspectives*, ed. Agneta H. Fischer (Cambridge University Press, 2000), 254–76, https://doi.org/10.1017/CBO9780511628191.013.

3 Harry Stack Sullivan, *The Interpersonal Theory of Psychiatry* (W. W. Norton & Co., 1953), 17.

4 Elinor Cleghorn, *Unwell Women: A Journey Through Medicine and Myth in a Man-Made World* (Dutton, 2021), 168.

5   Caitlyn Collins, "Is Maternal Guilt a Cross-National Experience?" *Qualitative Sociology* 44, no. 2 (2021): 1–29, https://doi.org/10.1007/s11133-020 -09451-2.

6   Robert Sterner et al., "The Conservation of Mass," *Nature Education Knowledge* 3, no. 10 (2011): 20.

Chapter 3: The Four Furies of Unreasonable Expectations

1   Donald W. Winnicott, *Playing & Reality* (Tavistock Publications, 1971), 7.

2   Randy Frost et al., "The Dimensions of Perfectionism," *Cognitive Therapy and Research* 14, no. 5 (1990): 449–68, https://doi.org/10.1007/BF0117 2967.

3   Thomas Curran and Andrew Hill, "Perfectionism Is Increasing over Time: A Meta-Analysis of Birth Cohort Differences from 1989 to 2016," *Psychological Bulletin* 145, no. 4 (2019): 410–29, http://dx.doi.org/10.1037 /bul0000138.

4   James Griffith, "Hope Modules: Brief Psychotherapeutic Interventions to Counter Demoralization from Daily Stressors of Chronic Illness," *Academic Psychiatry* 42 (February 2018): 135–45, https://doi.org/10.1007 /s40596-017-0748-7; Martin M. Smith et al., "Are Perfectionism Dimensions Vulnerability Factors for Depressive Symptoms After Controlling for Neuroticism? A Meta-Analysis of 10 Longitudinal Studies," *European Journal of Personality* 30, no. 2 (2016): 201–12, https://doi.org/10.1002 /per.2053.

5   Ansley M. Bender et al., "Perfectionism, Negative Life Events, and Cognitive Appraisal: A Contextual Model of Perfectionism's Maladaptive Nature," *Journal of Rational-Emotive & Cognitive-Behavioral Therapy* 40, no. 4 (2022): 723–42, https://doi.org/10.1007/s10942-021-00437-9.

6   Lenny R. Vartanian and Joshua M. Smyth, "Primum Non Nocere: Obesity Stigma and Public Health," *Journal of Bioethical Inquiry* 10, no. 1 (2013): 49–57, https://doi.org/10.1007/s11673-012-9412-9; Eric Robinson et al., "Self-Perception of Overweight and Obesity: A Review of Mental and Physical Health Outcomes," *Obesity Science and Practice* 6, no. 5 (2020): 552–61, https://doi.org/10.1002/osp4.424.

7   Joachim Stoeber and Laura N. Harvey, "Multidimensional Sexual Perfectionism and Female Sexual Function: A Longitudinal Investigation," *Archives of Sexual Behavior* 45, no. 8 (2016): 2003–14, https://doi.org/10.1007 /s10508-016-0721-7.

8   Ea Høg Utoft, "'All the Single Ladies' as the Ideal Academic During Times of COVID-19?" *Gender, Work & Organization* 27, no. 5 (2020): 778–87, https://doi.org/10.1111/gwao.12478.

Chapter 4: Why Guilt Is So Sticky— and How We Can Get Unstuck

1   Juliana G. Breines and Serena Chen, "Self-Compassion Increases Self-Improvement Motivation," *Personality and Social Psychology Bulletin* 38, no. 9 (2012): 1120–44, https://doi.org/10.1177/0146167212445599.
2   Trisha L. Raque et al., "Pathways by Which Self-Compassion Improves Positive Body Image: A Qualitative Analysis," *Behavioral Sciences* 13, no. 11 (2023): 939, https://doi.org/10.3390/bs13110939.
3   Kristin Neff, "Self-Compassion: An Alternative Conceptualization of a Healthy Attitude Toward Oneself," *Self and Identity* 2, no. 2 (2003): 85–101, https://doi.org/10.1080/15298860309032.

Chapter 5: Identifying Your Guilt Triggers

1   Paul Rozin and Edward B. Royzman, "Negativity Bias, Negativity Dominance, and Contagion," *Personality and Social Psychology Review* 5, no. 4 (2001): 296–320, https://doi.org/10.1207/S15327957PSPR0504_2.
2   Eric Kandel, *In Search of Memory: The Emergence of a New Science of Mind* (W. W. Norton & Company, 2007).
3   Tricia Padoa et al., "Comparative Social Media Use and the Mental Health of Mothers with High Levels of Perfectionism," *Journal of Social and Clinical Psychology* 37, no. 7 (2018): 514–35, https://doi.org/10.1521/jscp.2018.37.7.514.

Chapter 6: Quieting Your Guilty Thoughts

1   Aaron T. Beck et al., *Cognitive Therapy of Depression* (Guilford Publications, 1987).
2   Carol Dweck, *Mindset: The New Psychology of Success* (Random House, 2006).
3   Martin E. P. Seligman et al., "Positive Psychology Progress: Empirical Validation of Interventions," *American Psychologist* 60, no. 5 (2005): 410–21, https://doi.org/10.1037/0003-066X.60.5.410.

Notes

4 Fred B. Bryant and Joseph Veroff, *Savoring: A New Model of Positive Experience* (Lawrence Erlbaum Associates, 2007).
5 Mihaly Csikszentmihalyi, *Flow: The Psychology of Optimal Experience* (Harper Perennial, 1991).
6 Edith Hall, *Aristotle's Way: How Ancient Wisdom Can Change Your Life* (Penguin Press, 2019).
7 "VIA Survey of Character," Authentic Happiness, University of Pennsylvania, https://www.authentichappiness.sas.upenn.edu.

Chapter 7: Engaging with Agency

1 Vivek H. Murthy, *Together: The Healing Power of Human Connection in a Sometimes Lonely World* (Harper Wave, 2020).
2 Myrna M. Weissman et al., *Comprehensive Guide to Interpersonal Psychotherapy* (Basic Books, 2000).
3 Sasha K. Shillcutt and Julie K. Sliver, "Social Media and Advancement of Women Physicians," *New England Journal of Medicine* 378, no. 24 (2018): 2342–45, https://www.doi.org/10.1056/NEJMms1801980.